YOUTH PRAISE

numbers 1 - 299

FALCON BOOKS LONDON

This is a reprint of the words editions of *Youth Praise 1* and *Youth Praise 2*, the music editions of which are published separately. Music edition of nos. 1–150 first published 1966, words edition first published 1968; nos. 151–299 first published in music and words editions 1969; first issued in this format 1972, reprinted 1972, 1974, 1975.

SBN 85491 086 7

Published by the
Church Pastoral Aid Society
Falcon Court, 32 Fleet Street, London EC4Y 1DB

Cover by M G O Graphics

Printed by Billing & Sons Limited,
Guildford and London

YOUTH PRAISE 1

1

We will sing of our Redeemer, He's our King:
All His glory, all His praise to you we bring;
With our hearts and with our voices Him we sing,
We love the Lord, we love His Word, He's our
    King.

© L. C. Barnes and G. Brattle *By kind permission*

2

Start with chorus
Come and praise the Lord our King, Hallelujah.
Come and praise the Lord our King, Hallelujah.

1 Christ was born in Bethlehem, Hallelujah,
   Son of God and Son of Man, Hallelujah:
   Chorus

2 He grew up an earthly child, Hallelujah,
   Of the world, but undefiled, Hallelujah:
   Chorus

3 Jesus died at Calvary, Hallelujah,
   Rose again triumphantly, Hallelujah:
   Chorus

4 He will cleanse us from our sin, Hallelujah,
   If we live by faith in Him, Hallelujah:
   Chorus

5 We will live with Him one day, Hallalujah,
   And for ever with Him stay, Hallelujah:
   Chorus

© I. Bowman *By kind permission*

3

1   Tell out, my soul, the greatness of the Lord;
    Unnumbered blessings give my spirit voice;
    Tender to me the promise of His Word;
    In God my Saviour shall my heart rejoice.

2   Tell out, my soul, the greatness of His Name!
    Make known His might, the deeds His arm has
      done;
    His mercy sure, from age to age the same;
    His Holy Name—the Lord, the Mighty One.

3   Tell out, my soul, the greatness of His might!
    Powers and dominions lay their glory by.
    Proud hearts and stubborn wills are put to flight,
    The hungry fed, the humble lifted high.

4   Tell out, my soul, the glories of His Word!
    Firm is His promise, and His mercy sure.
    Tell out, my soul, the greatness of the Lord
    To children's children and for evermore!

© T. Dudley-Smith 1962   *By kind permission*

4

There's no greater Name than Jesus,
Name of Him who came to save us,
In that saving Name of Jesus
Every knee should bow.

Let ev'rything that is 'neath the ground,
Let ev'rything in the world around,
Let ev'rything that's high o'er the sky
Bow at Jesus' Name.

In our minds by faith professing,
In our hearts by inward blessing,
On our tongues by words confessing,
Jesus Christ is Lord!

© M. A. Baughen 1964   *By kind permission*

5

1 When morning gilds the skies,
   My heart awaking cries,
   'May Jesus Christ be praised!'
   Alike at work and prayer
   To Jesus I repair:
   'May Jesus Christ be praised!'

2 Be this, when day is past,
   Of all my thoughts the last,
   'May Jesus Christ be praised!'
   The night becomes as day,
   When from the heart we say:
   'May Jesus Christ be praised!'

3 Does sadness fill my mind,
   A solace here I find,
   'May Jesus Christ be praised!'
   When evil thoughts molest,
   With this I shield my breast:
   'May Jesus Christ be praised!'

4 To God, the Word on high,
   The hosts of angels cry,
   'May Jesus Christ be praised!'
   Let mortals, too, upraise
   Their voice in hymns of praise:
   'May Jesus Christ be praised!'

5 Let earth's wide circle round
   In joyful notes resound,
   'May Jesus Christ be praised!'
   Let earth and sea and sky,
   From depth to height, reply:
   'May Jesus Christ be praised!'

6 Be this while life is mine
   My canticle divine,
   'May Jesus Christ be praised!'
   Be this the eternal song,
   Through all the ages long:
   'May Jesus Christ be praised!'

6

There is joy in the presence of the angels of God
Over one sinner that repenteth.
There is joy in the presence of the angels of God
Over one sinner that repenteth.
For the Son of Man is come to seek,
To seek and to save that which was lost.
There is joy in the presence of the angels of God
Over one sinner that repenteth,
Praise the Lord for His love and for His heaven above,
Where His saints shall rejoice for ever.

7

1   I'm singing for my Lord everywhere I go,
Singing of His wondrous love that the world may
know
How He saved a wretch like me by His death on
Calvary,
I'm singing for my Lord everywhere I go.

2   I'm singing, but sometimes heavy is the rod,
For this world is not a friend to the grace of God;
Yet I sing the whole day long, for He fills my heart
with song,
I'm singing for my Lord everywhere I go.

3   I'm singing for the lost just because I know
Jesus Christ, whose precious blood washes white
as snow;
If my songs to Him can bring some lost soul I'll
gladly sing:
I'm singing for my Lord everywhere I go.

4   I'm singing, for the saints as they journey home;
Soon they'll reach that happy land where they'll
never roam,
And with me they'll join and sing praises to our
Lord and King:
I'm singing for my Lord everywhere I go.

8

Sweet is the work, my God, my King,
To praise Thy Name, give thanks and sing,
To show Thy love by morning light,
And talk of all Thy truth at night.

© Joshua Duckworth Ltd, Colne, Lancs *By kind permission*

9

1 We sing a loving Jesus
   Who left His throne above
   And came to earth to ransom
   The children of His love;
   It is an oft-told story,
   And yet we love to tell
   How Christ, the King of glory
   Once deigned with man to dwell.

2 We sing a lowly Jesus
   No kingly crown He had
   His heart was bowed with anguish
   His face was marred and sad;
   In deep humiliation
   He came, His work to do;
   O Lord of our salvation
   Let us be humble too.

3 We sing a mighty Jesus
   Whose voice could raise the dead
   The sightless eyes He opened
   The famished souls He fed.
   Thou camest to deliver
   Mankind from sin and shame;
   Redeemer and life-giver,
   We praise Thy Holy Name!

4 We sing a coming Jesus
   The time is drawing near
   When Christ with all His angels
   In glory shall appear.
   Lord, save us, we entreat Thee,
   In this Thy day of grace,
   That we may gladly meet Thee,
   And see Thee face to face.

10

1 Christ triumphant ever reigning,
    Saviour, Master, King,
    Lord of heav'n, our lives sustaining,
    Hear us as we sing.
    Yours the glory and the crown—
    The high renown—
    The eternal name.

2 Word incarnate, truth revealing,
    Son of Man on earth,
    Power and majesty concealing
    By Your humble birth.
    Yours the glory and the crown—
    The high renown—
    The eternal name.

3 Suffering servant, scorned, ill-treated,
    Victim crucified,
    Death is through the cross defeated
    Sinners justified.
    Yours the glory and the crown—
    The high renown—
    The eternal name.

4 Priestly King, enthroned for ever
    High in heaven above,
    Sin and death and hell shall never
    Stifle hymns of love.
    Yours the glory and the crown—
    The high renown—
    The eternal name.

5 So, our hearts and voices raising
    Through the ages long,
    Ceaselessly upon You gazing
    This shall be our song.
    Yours the glory and the crown—
    The high renown—
    The eternal name.

© M. Saward 1964 *By kind permission*

11

1 Lord of the cross of shame,
Set my cold heart aflame
With love for You, my Saviour and my Master;
Who on that lonely day
Bore all my sins away,
And saved me from the judgement and disaster.

2 Lord of the empty tomb,
Born of a virgin's womb,
Triumphant over death, its power defeated;
How gladly now I sing
Your praise, my risen King,
And worship You, in heaven's splendour seated.

3 Lord of my life today,
Teach me to live and pray
As one who knows the joy of sins forgiven;
So may I ever be,
Now and eternally,
United with the citizens of heaven.

© M. Saward 1964 *By kind permission*

12

1 He who now is reigning in majesty
Stooped to bear our sin in humility,
There on Calvary—Jesus died for me—
Died to set me free—eternally!

　　Chorus
　　Jesus Christ is my Lord and King,
　　To Him honour and glory bring,
　　Join the mighty host in heav'n above
　　　　and praise His gracious Name.

2 Justified by faith we have peace with God,
Fellowship with Him through our Saviour's blood,
Wonder though it be—sons of God are we—
In His family—eternally!
　　Chorus

© M. A. Baughen *By kind permission*

13

Thank You for ev'ry new good morning,
Thank You for ev'ry fresh new day,
Thank You that I may cast my burdens
Wholly onto You.

Thank You for ev'ry friend I have, Lord,
Thank You for ev'ryone I know,
Thank You when I can feel forgiveness
To my greatest foe.

Thank You for leisure and employment,
Thank You for ev'ry heartfelt joy,
Thank You for all that makes me happy
And for melody.

Thank You for ev'ry shade and sorrow,
Thank You for comfort in Your Word,
Thank You that I am guided by You
Ev'rywhere I go.

Thank You for grace to know Your gospel,
Thank You for all Your Spirit's power,
Thank You for Your unfailing love which
Reaches far and near.

Thank You for free and full salvation,
Thank You for grace to hold it fast,
Thank You, O Lord, I want to thank You,
That I'm free to thank!

14

Oh, thank the Lord, oh thank the Lord,
Give Him the praise for He is good;
Because His mercy does endure,
His faithfulness is ever sure;
Oh thank the Lord, oh thank the Lord,
Give Him the praise for He is good.

15

1 O Lord most high, Thou holy God and Saviour,
Thy pow'r and might are more than tongue can tell,
But greater far the love that planned salvation
And saved the lost from sin and death and hell.

Chorus
O God of Love, O God of Calvary,
How great Thou art! How great Thou art!
In all the world there is no one like Thee,
How great Thou art! How great Thou art!

2 Once far from God, an alien and a stranger,
Of hope bereft, a sinner lost and lone,
But Jesus came to rescue from the danger,
To give us life He sacrificed His own.
Chorus

3 In mercy rich, in love and grace abounding,
When we were dead in trespasses and sins,
Thine only Son for us was freely given,
How great Thou art! in Thee our life begins.
Chorus

© Words and Arrangement by Norman J. Clayton 1957
Used by kind permission of Rodeheaver Co., U.S.A.

16

Open Thou my eyes, O Lord,
Open Thou my eyes, O Lord;
That I may see the wondrous things of Thy law,
Wondrous things of Thy law,
Wondrous things of Thy law
Open Thou my eyes.

© G. R. Timms 1964 *By kind permission*

17

Lord, You look with goodness on us,
Lord, You pour Your love upon us,
And You promise in Your Word
To hear us when we pray.

© Gustav Bosse Verlag, Germany *By kind permission*

18

Come among us, Lord
Gathered round Thy Word,
To mind and heart Thy truth impart
O living Word.
In this morning (evening) hour,
Lord, reveal Thy power!
May souls be fed with living bread:
Come among us, Lord!

© G. Brattle   *By kind permission*

19

By blue Galilee Jesus walked of old,
By blue Galilee wondrous things He told.
Saviour, still my teacher be,
Showing wondrous things to me,
As of old by Galilee, blue Galilee.

© The Venturers   *By kind permission*

20

Turn your eyes upon Jesus,
Look full in His wonderful face;
And the things of earth will grow strangely dim
In the light of His glory and grace.

© 1922, renewal 1950 by H. H. Lemmel
Assigned to Singspiration Inc. All rights reserved
By kind permission

21

Break Thou the Bread of Life, dear Lord, to me,
As Thou didst break the loaves beside the sea;
Beyond the sacred page I seek Thee, Lord;
My spirit longs for Thee, O living Word!

22

Speak to us, Lord, in this brief hour today;
Give light upon the written word we pray;
Stir heart and mind to heed and to obey,
For this we plead.

© G. Brattle   *By kind permission*

23

Triumphant victor, life-giving Saviour,
Ris'n from the dead on that first Easter day.
Make known Thy power, Lord, to each one here, Lord,
Thou risen Son of God, we own Thy sway.

24

God's love is wonderful, God's love is wonderful,
Wonderful that He should give His Son to die for me,
God's love is wonderful.

25

On Calv'ry's tree He died for me,
That I His love might know.
To set me free He died for me,
That's why I love Him so.

26

1 Wonderful grace of Jesus, greater than all my sin;
   How shall my tongue describe it, where shall its
     praise begin?
   Taking away my burden, setting my spirit free,
   For the wonderful grace of Jesus reaches me.

   Chorus
   Wonderful the matchless grace of Jesus,
   Deeper than the mighty rolling sea:
   Higher than the mountain, sparkling like a
     fountain,
   All sufficient grace for even me.
   Broader than the scope of my transgressions,
   Greater far than all my sin and shame
   Oh, magnify the precious Name of Jesus
   Praise His Name!

2 Wonderful grace of Jesus, reaching to all the lost;
   By it I have been pardoned, saved to the uttermost,
   Chains have been torn asunder, giving me liberty,
   For the wonderful grace of Jesus reaches me:
      Chorus

3 Wonderful grace of Jesus, reaching the most defiled,
   By its transforming power, making him God's own
      child,
   Purchasing peace and heaven, for all eternity,
   And the wonderful grace of Jesus reaches me:
      Chorus

27

Higher than the hills, deeper than the sea,
Broader than the skies above is my Redeemer's love
   for me;
To His cross of shame, Jesus freely came,
Bearing all my sin and sorrow—Wondrous love!

28

1 In the garden Gethsemane
   Christ Jesus knelt alone;
   With burdened heart and pain ahead
   He faced the cross alone;
   Never was a man forsaken
   In such a way as this:
   In the garden Gethsemane
   Christ Jesus knelt alone.

2 In the garden Gethsemane
   Christ Jesus knelt alone,
   Yet where were His disciples when
   He faced the cross alone?
   Eyes were heavy, sleep was easy,
   They let Him watch alone
   In the garden Gethsemane:
   Christ Jesus knelt alone.

3 In the garden Gethsemane
   Christ Jesus knelt alone,
   'Father', He said, 'Thy will be done'
   Christ Jesus knelt alone;
   Then the cross for our salvation
   For us then to atone:
   In the garden Gethsemane
   Christ Jesus knelt alone.

4 In the garden Gethsemane
   Christ Jesus knelt alone,
   And now today He looks to us
   To those He calls His own;
   Are we watching? Are we praying?
   Or are we failing Him?
   In the garden Gethsemane
   Christ Jesus knelt alone.

29

The grace of the Lord, like a fathomless sea,
Sufficient for you, sufficient for me,
Is tender and patient and boundless and free
Sufficient for ev'ry need.

30

Living, He loved me;
Dying, He saved me;
Buried, He carried my sins far away;
Rising, He justified
Freely for ever;
One day He's coming,
O glorious day!

31

For God so loved the world, He gave His only Son,
To die on Calvary's tree, from sin to set me free;
Some day He's coming back, what glory that will be,
Wonderful His love to me.

32

1   It was just two thousand years ago
    He walked thro' Galilee,
    The eternal God had stepped below
    In human form to be;
    Born of a lowly Hebrew maid,
    A carpenter He was by trade;
    He came down,
    Two thousand years ago:

      Chorus

      They tell of Jesus' glory,
      Who met Him in the way;
      And it is no idle story,
      For He lives in me today;
      He gives me peace and purpose true,
      A power that's old, but ever new;
      God came down,
      Two thousand years ago.

2   It was just two thousand years ago
    He died on Calvary;
    It was for sin He suffered so,
    Though innocent was He.
    My sin and guilt lay on His head;
    My penalty He bore instead;
    He suffered,
    Two thousand years ago:

      Chorus

3   It was just two thousand years ago
    An empty tomb was found;
    The stone was rolled away we know,
    The powers of hell are bound;
    My risen Lord is now on high,
    He lives that we may never die,
    He triumphed!
    Two thousand years ago:

      Chorus

33

Oh, the love that drew salvation's plan!
Oh, the grace that brought it down to man!
Oh, the mighty gulf that God did span at Calvary!
Mercy there was great, and grace was free;
Pardon there was multiplied to me;
There my burdened soul found liberty, at Calvary.

34

1   Just because He set His heart on me,
    Just because His pow'r could set me free,
    Just because of my iniquity
    Jesus died.

2   When by Him the ransom was supplied,
    When by Him the debt was satisfied,
    When by Him we could be justified
    Jesus rose.

3   Now of Calvary each Christian sings,
    Now with praise to Christ all heaven rings,
    Now He's Lord of Lords and King of Kings
    Jesus reigns.

© A. E. Kelly   *By kind permission*

35

His compassions fail not, fail not,
His compassions fail not, they are new ev'ry morning,
Great is Thy faithfulness, great is Thy faithfulness;
His compassions fail not, they are new ev'ry day.

© G. R. Timms 1964   *By kind permission*

36

1   Can it be true, the things they say of You?
    You walked this earth sharing with friends You
       knew
    All that they had the work, the joy, the pain,
    That we might find the way to heav'n again.

2   And day by day You still return this way;
    But we recall there was a debt to pay:
    Out of Your love for Your own world above,
    You left that holy thing, Your endless love to prove.

3   Can it be true, the things they did to You –
    The death, the shame, and were Your friends so
        few?
    Yet You returned again alive and free –
    Can it be true, my Lord, it had to be.

© Brother William SSF   *By kind permission*

37

I know a fount where sins are wash'd away;
I know a place where night is turned to day;
Burdens are lifted, blind eyes made to see:
There's a wonder working pow'r in the blood of
    Calvary.

© The Salvation Army International Music Board
By kind permission

38

1   Tell me Lord Jesus;
    Why did You have to die, Master?
    Tell me Lord Jesus:
    Why did You have to die?

        Chorus
        And You came down to earth,
        From heaven willingly,
        There at Calvary.
        On the cursed tree,
        There You died for me,
        There You died for me.

2   Pride, sin and wrong in us,
    That cut us off from God, our Father,
    When we were bound in sin,
    That's when You came to die.
        Chorus

3 You came to set us free,
   That's why You had to die, Master,
   To give us liberty,
   That's why You had to die.
        Chorus

39

1 New! ev'ry morning it's new!
   The love of God to me is wonderfully new!
   New! ev'ry morning it's new!
   The mercy of the Lord is wonderfully new!
   Great is His faithfulness, constant is His love,
   Great is His saving pow'r coming from above.

2 New! ev'ry morning it's new!
   The love of Calvary is wonderfully new!
   New! ev'ry morning it's new!
   The mercy fresh outpoured is wonderfully new!
   He is our daily strength, He's our daily guide
   If we will wait on Him and in Him abide!

3 New! ev'ry morning it's new!
   The love of God to me is wonderfully new!
   New! ev'ry morning it's new!
   The mercy of the Lord is wonderfully new!

40

1 Jesu, lover of my soul,
   Let me to Thy bosom fly,
   While the nearer waters roll,
   While the tempest still is high,
   Hide me, O my Saviour, hide,
   Till the storm of life is past;
   Safe into the haven guide;
   O receive my soul at last!

2 Other refuge have I none;
   Hangs my helpless soul on Thee;
   Leave, ah, leave me not alone;
   Still support and comfort me.
   All my trust on Thee is stayed;
   All my help from Thee I bring;
   Cover my defenceless head
   With the shadow of Thy wing.

3 Thou, O Christ, art all I want;
   More than all in Thee I find;
   Raise the fallen, cheer the faint,
   Heal the sick and lead the blind.
   Just and holy is Thy name,
   I am all unrighteousness;
   False and full of sin I am,
   Thou art full of truth and grace.

4 Plenteous grace with Thee is found,
   Grace to cover all my sin;
   Let the healing streams abound;
   Make and keep me pure within.
   Thou of life the fountain art,
   Freely let me take of Thee;
   Spring Thou up within my heart,
   Rise to all eternity.

41

1 Ride on, ride on in majesty!
   Hark, all the tribes Hosanna cry;
   O Saviour meek, pursue Thy road
   With palms and scattered garments strowed.

2 Ride on, ride on in majesty!
   In lowly pomp ride on to die;
   O Christ, Thy triumphs now begin
   O'er captive death and conquered sin.

3 Ride on, ride on in majesty!
   The angel armies of the sky
   Look down with sad and wondering eyes
   To see the approaching sacrifice.

4 Ride on, ride on in majesty!
   Thy last, Thy fiercest strife is nigh;
   The Father on His sapphire throne
   Awaits His own anointed Son.

5 Ride on, ride on in majesty!
   In lowly pomp ride on to die;
   Bow Thy meek head to mortal pain,
   Then take, O God, Thy power, and reign.

42

Jesus died for me, His blood has made me free.
Now He lives within me and He leads the way;
While I trust in Him I've vict'ry over sin:
Praise His Name He loves me so, and He shall be my
   King.

© G. R. Timms 1964 *By kind permission*

43

1 There is a Name I love to hear,
   I love to speak its worth;
   It sounds like music in my ear,
   The sweetest Name on earth:

   Chorus
   Oh, how I love the Saviour's Name
   Oh, how I love the Saviour's Name,
   Oh, how I love the Saviour's Name,
   The sweetest Name on earth.

2 It tells me of a Saviour's love,
   Who died to set me free;
   It tells me of His precious blood,
   The sinner's perfect plea:
      Chorus

3 It tells of one whose loving heart
   Can feel my deepest woe,
   Who in my sorrow bears a part
   That none can bear below:
      Chorus

4 It bids my trembling heart rejoice,
   It dries each rising tear;
   It tells me in a 'still, small voice'
   To trust and never fear:
      Chorus

5 Jesus, the Name I love so well,
   The Name I love to hear!
   No saint on earth its worth can tell,
   No heart conceive how dear!
      Chorus

44

Christ for me, yes, it's Christ for me,
He's my Saviour, my Lord and King;
I'm so happy I shout and sing;
Ev'ry day as I go my way it is Christ for me.

45

1 The Saviour has come in His mighty pow'r,
   And spoken peace to my soul,
   And all of my life from that very hour
   I've yielded to His control,
   I've yielded to His control.

      Chorus
      Wonderful, wonderful, Marvellous and wonderful,
      What He has done for my soul!
      The half has never been told;
      Oh, It is wonderful, It is marvellous and wonderful,
      What Jesus has done for this soul of mine!
      The half has never been told!

2 From glory to glory He leads me on,
   From grace to grace ev'ry day,
   And brighter and brighter the glory dawns
   While pressing my homeward way,
   While pressing my homeward way.
      Chorus

3 If fellowship here with my Lord can be
   So inexpressibly sweet,
   O what will it be when His face we see,
   When round the white throne we meet,
   When round the white throne we meet?
        Chorus

46

1 There's a psalm of praise filling all my days,
   Since to Jesus my heart did bow;
   O what melody! Glorious harmony!
   Life is wonderful now:

   Chorus
   Life is wonderful, Yes, it's wonderful!
   Life is wonderful now to me!
   I let Jesus in, He changed ev'rything,
   Life is wonderful now!
   Since His blessings came into my heart
   Joy unspeakable fills ev'ry part,
   And I want to live for my Lord;
   Life is wonderful now!

2 All is happiness, gone is my distress,
   Peace and vict'ry He does endow;
   Since my Saviour came, I can't be the same;
   Life is wonderful now:
        Chorus

3 All my life is praise for His wondrous grace,
   I will serve the Lord, this my vow;
   Jesus came to me, and He set me free;
   Life is wonderful now:
        Chorus

47

Jesus came from heaven with a humble birth,
Took man's form upon Him to live with us on earth.
Jesus grew to manhood in God's perfect plan,
Told us of His Father and His great love for man.
Jesus died at Calv'ry to wash my sins away,
Now He reigns in glory on high.
Jesus lives within me all along life's way,
Jesus came from heaven for me!

48

In my need Jesus found me,
Put His strong arm around me,
Brought me safe home,
Into the shelter of the fold.
Gracious shepherd that sought me,
Precious life-blood that brought me
Out of the night,
Into the light, and nigh to God.

49

Gone! Gone! Gone! Gone! Yes, my sins are gone.
Now my soul is free and in my heart's a song.
Buried in the deepest sea.
Yes, that's good enough for me.
I shall live eternally.
Praise God! my sins are gone.

50

I'm not ashamed, not ashamed of the gospel of Christ
For it is the pow'r of God unto salvation
To ev'ryone, to ev'ryone that believeth.

51

Joined to the vine as a branch of the tree,
Cleansed by His word that He's spoken to me,
Stemmed in His love as He wants me to be:
Bearing the fruit of the Lord.

52

He lives! He lives! Christ Jesus lives today!
He walks with me and talks with me along life's narrow
    way.
He lives! He lives, salvation to impart!
You ask me how I know He lives – He lives within my
    heart.

53

Thou shalt guide me with Thy counsel
And after that receive me with glory.
Whom have I in heav'n but Thee,
And who on earth more dear to me?
Thou shalt guide me with Thy counsel
And after that receive me with glory.

54

1 Jesus my Lord will love me for ever,
   From Him no pow'r of evil can sever
   He gave His life to ransom my soul,
   Now I belong to Him:

      Chorus
      Now I belong to Jesus,
      Jesus belongs to me,
      Not for the years of time alone,
      But for eternity.

2 Once I was lost in sin's degradation,
 Jesus came down to bring me salvation,
 Lifted me up from sorrow and shame,
 Now I belong to Him:
   Chorus

3 Joy floods my soul for Jesus has saved me,
 Freed me from sin that long had enslaved me,
 His precious blood He gave to redeem,
 Now I belong to Him:
   Chorus

55

1 Who can cheer the heart like Jesus,
 By His presence all divine?
 True and tender, pure and precious,
 O how blest to call Him mine!

   Chorus
   All that thrills my soul is Jesus;
   He is more than life to me, (to me),
   And the fairest of ten thousand
   In my blessed Lord I see.

2 Love of Christ so freely given,
 Grace of God beyond degree,
 Mercy higher than the heaven,
 Deeper than the deepest sea:
   Chorus

3 What a wonderful redemption!
 Never can a mortal know
 How my sin, tho' red like crimson,
 Can be whiter than the snow:
   Chorus

4 Ev'ry need His hand supplying,
 Ev'ry good in Him I see;
 On His strength divine relying,
 He is all in all to me:
   Chorus

5   By the crystal flowing river
    With the ransom'd I will sing,
    And for ever and for ever
    Praise and glorify the King:
        Chorus

56

Things are diff'rent now, something happened to me
When I gave my heart to Jesus.

Things are diff'rent now; I was chang'd, it must be,
When I gave my heart to Him.

Things I loved before have passed away,
Things I love far more have come to stay.

57

(*Fellows*): It's an open secret, that Jesus is mine,
        (*Girls*): Open secret, Jesus is mine;
(*Fellows*): It's an open secret, this gladness divine;
        (*Girls*): Open secret, gladness divine;
(*Fellows*): It's an open secret, I want you to know;
        (*Girls*): Secret, secret, Want you to
                know;
(*Fellows*): It's an open secret, I love my Saviour so.
        (*Girls*): Secret, O I love Him so.

And you can seek Him, find Him, Share this secret, too;
Know His loving kindness in ev'rything you do.

(*Fellows*): It's an open secret, I want you to know;
        (*Girls*): Secret, secret, want you to
                know;
(*Fellows*): It's an open secret,
        (*Girls*): secret,
I love my Saviour so! so!
Love my Saviour so!

58

1 I would love to tell you what I think of Jesus.
   Since I found in Him a Friend so strong and true;
   I would tell how you He chang'd my life completely.
   He did something that no other friend could do.

   Chorus
   No one ever cared for me like Jesus.
   There's no other friend so kind as He;
   No one else could take the sin and darkness from
   *   me*
   O how much He cared for me.

2 All my life was full of sin when Jesus found me,
   All my heart was full of misery and woe;
   Jesus placed His strong and loving arms about me,
   And He led me in the way I ought to go:
   *   Chorus*

3 Ev'ry day He comes to me with new assurance,
   More and more I understand His words of love;
   But I'll never know just why He came to save me
   Till some day I see His blessed face above:
   *   Chorus*

© Rodeheaver Hall-Mack Co. *By kind permission*

59

He gives me satisfying peace, this wonderful Saviour.
He gives me joys that never cease, this wonderful Lord.
'Tis only Jesus who can bless with everlasting happiness,
And He's my Saviour, this wonderful Lord.

© N. J. Clayton 1943 *By kind permission*

60

Jesus is a wonderful Saviour, He will carry you thro',
Jesus is a wonderful Saviour, He will carry you thro',
   my brother;
Jesus is a wonderful Saviour, He will carry you thro',

And when the battle is done and the victory's won,
My Lord will carry you thro'
And on that last day when you're facing your Maker
You'll need my Jesus to be your Saviour;
He'll ever hide you in the rock of ages,
The rock of ages that was cleft for you,
That was cleft for you.

61

1   Jesus is the Saviour whom I love to know,
    Heaven is the haven that I'm going to,
    Jesus is the captain who now leads my life;
    Unworthy as I am I know He came to save
    A sinner such as me, a sinner such as me
    He came to save from the grave.

    Chorus
    For God so loved the world that He gave
        His only begotten Son
    That whosoever believeth on Him should not
        perish
    But have everlasting life.

2   Sometimes when you're feeling all alone and blue,
    Jesus can come in and help to pull you through;
    Sometimes you just know that you need Jesus too,
    So come on sinner, come to Him, He died for you
    A sinner such as you, a sinner such as me
    He came to save from the grave:
        Chorus

3   Jesus is the Saviour whom I love to know,
    Heaven is the haven where I'm going to go;
    Jesus is the captain who now leads my life,
    Unworthy as I am I know He came to save
    A sinner such as me, a sinner such as me
    He came to save from the grave.

62

1 Days are filled with gladness, nights are filled with
    song,
Walking in the King's highway
And the world grows brighter, as we pass along,
Walking in the King's highway.

    Chorus
    Walking (yes I'm) walking in the King's highway,
    Walking in the King's highway (The King's high-
        way),
    To the place of many mansions I shall come at last,
    Walking in the King's highway.

2 Music from the homeland fills me with delight,
Walking in the King's highway;
Visions of the glory break upon my sight,
Walking in the King's highway.
    Chorus

3 Crowned with tender mercies, guarded by His love
Walking in the King's highway;
Jesus gives a foretaste of the joys above,
Walking in the King's highway.
    Chorus

© Rodeheaver Hall-Mack Co. *By kind permission*

63

1 The King of love my Shepherd is
Whose goodness faileth never,
I nothing lack if I am His
And He is mine for ever.

2 Where streams of living water flow
My ransomed soul He leadeth,
And where the verdant pastures grow
With food celestial feedeth.

3 Perverse and foolish oft I strayed,
But yet in love He sought me
And on His shoulder gently laid
And home, rejoicing, brought me.

4 In death's dark vale I fear no ill
   With Thee, dear Lord, beside me;
   Thy rod and staff my comfort still,
   Thy cross before to guide me.

5 Thou spread'st a table in my sight;
   Thy unction grace bestoweth;
   And O, what transport of delight
   From Thy pure chalice floweth!

6 And so through all the length of days
   Thy goodness faileth never;
   Good Shepherd, may I sing Thy praise
   Within Thy house for ever.

64

Rise up and walk! All pow'r is given unto Him,
He changes not, and sin shall not have vict'ry over you.
Rise up and walk! He is the Lord that healeth thee,
At His command thou shalt be free, Christ Jesus
   makes you whole!

© G. R. Timms 1964 *By kind permission*

65

1 There is full salvation through that precious Name:
         Jesus came – took our blame;
   There is full salvation through that precious Name:
         No other name like Jesus.

2 He gives fellowship and guidance all the way:
         As we pray – ev'ry day;
   He gives fellowship and guidance all the way:
         There is no friend like Jesus.

3 Death is swallowed up for all eternity:
         Death will be – victory!
   Death is swallowed up for all eternity:
         We trust a risen Jesus.

4   There is full salvation through that precious Name:
         Jesus came – took our blame;
    There is full salvation through that precious Name:
         No other name like Jesus.

66

Ho! ev'ryone that thirsts in life
Hear the offer of the Lord;
He is the one who satisfies –
Come of your own accord.
Let the wicked forsake his way
And the unrighteous his thoughts;
Let him return to the Lord our God
And he will find pardon and mercy abundantly!
Seek ye the Lord while He may be found,
Call on Him while He's near;
Find Him as Saviour Lord and King
Know Him by love instead of fear.

67

Behold I stand, I stand at the door and knock,
Behold I stand at the door and knock;
If any man will hear My voice let him open the door
And I will come in and sup with him
And he with Me.

68

'Behold I stand, I stand at the door and knock,
Behold I stand, I stand at the door and knock,
If any man will listen to My voice, and open that door
I will come in.'
         This is the invitation that Jesus gives to you,
         This is the promise of His Word and it is true.

When He comes in it's fellowship divine,
For I am His and He is mine;
When He comes in, then He will sup with me
Until that day His face I'll see.
    This is the invitation that Jesus gives to you,
    This is the promise of His word and it is true.
Behold He stands, He stands at the door and knocks,
Behold He stands, He stands at the door and knocks;
If any man will listen to His voice, and open that
    door –
He will come in.

© M. A. Baughen 1964 *By kind permission*

69

There's a way back to God from the dark paths of sin;
There's a door that is open and you may go in:
At Calvary's cross is where you begin,
When you come as a sinner to Jesus.

70

1   I heard the voice of Jesus say
    'Come unto Me and rest,
    Lay down, thou weary one, lay down
    Thy head upon My breast.'
    I came to Jesus as I was,
    Weary and worn and sad,
    I found in Him a resting place
    And He has made me glad.

2   I heard the voice of Jesus say,
    'Behold, I freely give
    The living water: thirsty one,
    Stoop down and drink, and live.'
    I came to Jesus and I drank
    Of that life-giving stream;
    My thirst was quenched, my soul revived,
    And now I live in Him.

3　I heard the voice of Jesus say,
　　'I am this dark world's light,
　　Look unto Me, thy morn shall rise,
　　And all thy days be bright.'
　　I looked to Jesus and I found
　　In Him my star, my sun;
　　And in that light of life I'll walk,
　　Till travelling days are done.

71

1　Broad is the way that leads man to
　　The place that's called destruction;
　　Narrow the way to life anew,
　　The way which few will walk on:

　　　　Chorus
　　　　Get on the road which leads you to God
　　　　Start at the cross of Jesus;
　　　　He is the way, the truth, and the life –
　　　　So trust Him, come and follow Jesus (Jesus).

2　God has prepared a place for all
　　Who trust in Christ as Saviour;
　　His promise is that at His call
　　We'll live with Him for ever:
　　　　Chorus

3　We can draw near to God in prayer,
　　Know Him as Friend and Father;
　　We can approach God without fear,
　　And know His love for ever:
　　　　Chorus

4　No other way to God is true,
　　No other way than Jesus,
　　No other way to God for you –
　　Jesus alone can save us:
　　　　Chorus

72

If you want joy, real joy, wonderful joy,
Let Jesus come into your heart.
If you want joy, real joy, wonderful joy,
Let Jesus come into your heart.
Your sins He'll take away,
Your night He'll turn to day,
Your heart He'll make over anew,
And then come in to stay.
If you want joy, real joy, wonderful joy,
Let Jesus come into your heart.

73

Jesus is knocking, patiently waiting,
Outside your heart's closed door.
Do not reject Him, simply accept Him,
Now and for evermore.

74

In Christ there is full salvation,
In Christ there is pow'r o'er sin,
And all who believe on Jesus
Receive His life within.
In Christ there is satisfaction,
In Christ there is joy and rest,
And each hungry soul in Christ made whole
Is ever blest.

75

'Take up the cross, thyself deny
Come boldly after Me.'
The Saviour calls: let us reply,
'Lord, I will follow Thee.'

'Take up the cross, deny yourself,
Come boldly after Me.'
The Saviour calls: Lord give us grace
To rise and follow Thee.

76

1 Which way are you choosing, the narrow or broad?
   You'll have to make up your mind.
   Just give up your own way and follow the Lord;
   Why don't you make up your mind?
   He died, the stranger of Galilee
   To bring salvation to you and me;
   A strong companion you'll prove Him to be,
   So won't you make up your mind?

2 Which crowd will you follow, the large or the small?
   Be sure to make up your mind.
   The cost is demanding, but hear Jesus call;
   Then come and make up your mind.
   Your friends may shun you unthinkingly,
   But Christ gives power and liberty;
   To life with purpose you'll find the key,
   When once you make up your mind!

3 On which are you resting, the Rock or the sand?
   You'd better make up your mind!
   With Christ as foundation your building will stand
   But have you made up your mind?
   Temptations and trials must come your way,
   The storms of Judgment will rage one day;
   Take Jesus and on Him your confidence stay
   Don't wait, but make up your mind!

4 O what will you do with the Saviour today?
   He bids you make up your mind.
   Repent and accept Him without delay,
   O sinner, make up your mind!
   Why stumble alone along the road?
   He'll sort your tangles, He'll take your load,
   And in your heart He will make His abode;
   It's time to make up your mind!

© R. T. Bewes 1964 *By kind permission*

77

1   O there's only one way to heaven, brother,
    And you'd better get on that road.
    For it leads from Calvary's rugged cross
    To the gates of the city of God.
    For other roads will lead astray
    So take the strait and narrow way;
    So you'd better get on that road,
    You'd better get on that road.

2   O there's only one way to heaven, brother,
    And you'd better get on that road;
    For salvation's free, not by works you see,
    It is the gift of God's love bestowed.
    Your sin on Christ was full laid,
    Its penalty is really paid:
    So you'd better get on that road,
    You'd better get on that road.

3   O there's only one way to heaven, brother,
    And you'd better get on that road;
    For Christ is the door and His word is the key
    To a home in that blest abode.
    He is the Truth, the Life, the Way,
    O trust Him now without delay;
    And you'd better get on that road;
    You'd better get on that road.

78

How long, how long before you come to the Saviour?
Oh sinner, tell me how long.
You know, yes you know you're lost,
And so to the Saviour you certainly must go.

Well, Jesus died on Calvary to save the lost like you and
    me;
But still you go on living that way:
Come on now, come under His sway.
So come along, you'll sing that new song, today
To Jesus come along.

79

1 Christian, are you running,
  Free from weight of sin,
  With the hope before you
  A crown of life to win?
  Or is your burden heavy,
  Each step like backward pace:
  How are you progressing
  In the Christian race?

2 Where as you are running
  Do you fix your eyes,
  Are they set on Jesus
  With faith that never dies?
  Or is your vision dazzled
  With idols on the way:
  How are you progressing
  In the race today?

3 Are you ever mindful
  Of watchers yet unseen,
  Saints of God before you
  Who in the race have been?
  Or are your thoughts still dwelling
  On things the world holds dear:
  How are you progressing –
  Keep the vision clear.

4 Christian, press thou onwards,
  Looking to the Lord,
  Think now how His life-blood
  Was for thy soul outpoured;
  Then leave all burdens with Him,
  O never drag that load,
  End the race rejoicing,
  In that blest abode.

80

1 As you travel along on the Jericho road.
  Does the world seem all wrong, and heavy your
    load?
  Just bring it to Christ, your sins all confess;
  On the Jericho road, your heart He will bless.

Chorus
On the Jericho road there's room for just two,
No more and no less, just Jesus and you;
Each burden He'll bear, each sorrow He'll share,
There's never a care, for Jesus is there.

2 On the Jericho road blind Bartimaeus sat,
   His life was a void, so empty and flat;
   But Jesus appeared, one word brought him sight,
   On the Jericho road, Christ banished his night.
   Chorus

3 O brother, to you this message I bring,
   Though hope may be gone, He'll cause you to sing;
   At Jesus' command sin's shackles must fall,
   On the Jericho road, will you answer His call?
   Chorus

81

1 If any man will follow, if any man will follow,
   If any man will follow after my Jesus:
   Let him deny himself, oh, let him take up his cross,
   And let him come and follow after my Lord!

      Whosoever will live for self will throw his life
         away,
      Christ gives life to all who follow Him –
      What is a man advantaged if he gains the whole
         wide world.
      And then loses his soul!

2 If any man will follow, if any man will follow,
   If any man will follow after my Jesus:
   Let him deny himself, oh, let him take up his cross,
   And let him come and follow after my Lord!

      Whosoever will be ashamed of Jesus and His
         words,
      In this sinful age in which we live,
      Jesus the King will be ashamed of him in that
         great day,
      When in glory He comes!

3   If any man will follow, if any man will follow,
     If any man will follow after my Jesus,
     Let him deny himself, oh, let him take up his cross,
     And let him come and follow after my Lord!
     Let him come and follow after my Lord.

82

1   I'm glad I'm a Christian,
     I'm trusting the Lord;
     I rest on God's promise
     Believing His Word.

2   The past is forgiven,
     And now I am free;
     A mansion in heaven
     Is waiting for me.

3   O come to Jesus,
     Your sins all confess;
     He's longing to clothe you
     In His righteousness.

4   Admit you're a sinner,
     Believe He is true;
     And when you have found Him
     Your life He'll renew.

83

1   Though the world has forsaken God,
     Treads a diff'rent path, lives a diff'rent way,
     I walk the road that the Saviour trod,
     And all may know I live under Jesus' sway:

     Chorus
     They are watching you, marking all you do,
     Hearing the things you say;
     Let them see the Saviour as He shines in you,
     Let His pow'r control you ev'ry day.

2 Men will look at the life I lead,
See the side I take, and the things I love;
They judge my Lord by my every deed –
Lord, set my affections on things above:
Chorus

3 When assailed in temptation's hour,
By besetting sins, by the fear of man,
Then I can know Jesus' mighty power,
And become like Him in His perfect plan:
Chorus

4 Here on earth people walk in night;
With no lamp to guide, they are dead in sin;
I know the Lord Who can give them light,
I live, yet not I, but Christ within:
Chorus

84

1 If you will follow Jesus
Deny yourself, take up the cross,
And come and follow the Saviour;
Deny yourself, take up the cross,
If you will follow the Lord.

2 If you will follow Jesus
All earthly gain becomes but loss,
If you will follow the Saviour;
All earthly gain becomes but loss
If you will follow the Lord.

3 If you will follow Jesus
You'll really find abundant life,
If you will follow the Saviour;
You'll really find abundant life,
If you will follow the Lord.

4 If you will follow Jesus
Step out in faith upon the way,
And come and follow the Saviour;
Step out in faith upon the way,
And come and follow the Lord.

85

1 There's a time when you travel way back in time;
   When you try to unravel, and upwards climb:
   Up above the sorrows and scares,
   In search of someone who cares,
   And you find that God cares for you. . .

   Chorus
   He'll see you through;
   If you think and pray, simply trust and say,
   Come and make my life be new.

2 The place your search leads you to has no escape;
   Up a hill to a cross it's true – a grim landscape:
   Calvary's the place you're in,
   Christ is dying for your sin,
   And you know that God cares for you. . .
     Chorus

3 Come with me up to His side and see His face;
   Kneel awhile, forget your pride and see His grace:
   Hear Him say 'Forgive them all',
   Now listen to His call,
   And you'll find that God cares for you. . .
     Chorus

4 It is hard for you to understand, but try you must;
   As a child takes his father's hand you must have
      trust:
   Trust in Christ – He died for you, –
   Believe in this – you know it's true,
   That God cares for you. . .
     Chorus

86

1 Not one precious promise of His Word
   Ever failed the servants of the Lord,
   Tried and proved by many like fine gold,
   Sweeter than the honey comb:

Chorus
Never doubt the Word,
God's own precious Word,
Never doubt the Word of God.
There's a promise true
In the Book for you,
Never doubt the Word of God.

2 Ev'ryone who takes God at His Word
   Need by doubters never be deterred,
   He will find the promise, read or heard,
   Never failing to be true:
      Chorus

3 Ev'ry promise can be yours or mine
   As to Him our minds in prayer incline,
   If our hearts have known His love divine
   We will want to love Him more:
      Chorus

© R. McCurdy Jones 1964 *By kind permission*

87

1 All Scriptures are given by the breath of God,
      Are inspired of God,
      Are the Word of the Lord;
   All Scriptures are given by the breath of God,
   And glorify His Name!

   They can make you wise to a saving faith
   In Jesus Christ the Lord;
   They can make the man of God complete,
   And are meant to be his sword!

2 So study to show yourself approved to God,
      Fit to use His Word,
      Fit to speak in His Name;
   So study to show yourself approved to God,
   A workman not ashamed.

   They'll reprove, correct, and a training in
   All righteous living afford;
   They will yield up all that we need to know
   Of teaching of the Lord!

3 All Scriptures are given by the breath of God,
     Are inspired of God,
     Are the Word of the Lord;
   All Scriptures are given by the breath of God,
   And glorify His Name!

© M. A. Baughen 1964 *By kind permission*

88

Before you start the day
Take time alone to pray,
And feed upon God's Word
To know His way;
So start the day with Him,
Then walk the way with Him,
And come to evening time with praise to Him.

© M. A. Baughen *By kind permission*

89

1 Lord, who left the highest heaven
   For a homeless human birth,
   And, a child within a stable,
   Came to share the life of earth
   With Thy grace and mercy bless
   All who suffer homelessness.

2 Lord, who sought by cloak of darkness
   Refuge under foreign skies
   From the swords of Herod's soldiers,
   Ravaged homes, and parents' cries –
   May Thy grace and mercy rest
   On the homeless and oppressed.

3 Lord, who lived secure and settled,
   Safe within the Father's plan,
   And in wisdom, stature, favour
   Growing up from boy to man –
   May Thy grace and mercy bless
   Us with growth in holiness.

4 Lord, who leaving home and kindred,
Followed still as duty led,
Sky the roof and earth the pillow
For the Prince of Glory's head –
With Thy grace and mercy bless
Sacrifice for righteousness.

5 Lord, who in Thy Cross and Passion
Helpless hung 'twixt earth and sky,
Yet whose thoughts were for Thy mother,
And a thief condemned to die –
May Thy grace and mercy rest
On the helpless and distressed.

6 Lord, who rose to life triumphant
With man's whole salvation won,
Risen, glorified, ascended,
All Thy Father's purpose done –
May Thy grace, all conflict past,
Bring Thy children home at last.

90

All your anxiety, all your care,
Bring to the mercy seat, leave it there.
Never a burden He cannot bear,
Never a friend like Jesus.

91

O Lord, teach me to pray,
As I believe on You.
O Lord, teach me to pray,
As I believe on You.
The words to tell you all I would
Are far too few
Lord, teach me to pray;
But I know You let us bring
Our ev'ry need to You.
Lord, teach us to pray!

92

God hears and He answers pray'r;
Cast on Jesus your ev'ry care,
Trust in His promises, they cannot fail,
For with the Father He'll ever prevail.
God hears and He answers pray'r,
Frees my spirit from all despair;
Hasten to take Him your problems.
For God answers prayer.

93

1   Trust in the Lord, and do not be discouraged,
    Trust in the Lord, and stop that feeling blue,
    Trust in the Lord and you will be encouraged,
    For Jesus cares for you.

2   Trust in the Lord, and not in any fable,
    Trust in the Lord, and find Him wholly true,
    Trust in the Lord, and know that He is able
    To fill your whole life through.

3   Trust in the Lord, and not in men or nation,
    Trust in the Lord, as Saviour, Lord, and King,
    Trust in the Lord for full and free salvation,
    And lift your heart and sing.

4   Trust in the Lord, faith is a great adventure,
    Trust in the Lord, and never cease to pray,
    Trust in the Lord, for all the unknown future,
    Today and every day!

© R. McCurdy Jones 1964   *By kind permission*

94

1   God's will for you is good,
    In the pattern of life
    Whatsoever each day may bring:
    Sing Him your song.

2   God's will for you is good,
    Ev'ry morning anew
    Think upon His great faithfulness:
    Sing Him your song.

3   God's will for you is good,
     Stop to ponder again
     All the blessings and gifts He gives:
     Sing Him your song.

4   God's will for you is good,
     Even sorrow and pain
     Can bring blessing through His grace:
     Sing Him your song.

5   God's will for you is good,
     For He sent His own Son
     To bear all our guilt and sin:
     Sing Him your song.

6   God's will for you is good,
     Be it sorrow or joy
     He is faithful in life and death:
     Sing Him your song.

95

1   I can do all things
     Through Christ the Lord who strengthens me;
     I can do all things
     Through Jesus Christ my King.
     For He is the strength of my heart and my soul,
     O Jesus, my Saviour;
     And He is my friend and my Lord and my all,
     O Jesus, my Lord.

2   I can do all things
     Through Christ my Lord who strengthens me;
     I can do all things
     Through Jesus Christ my King.
     I'm kept by the pow'r of His sheltering hand,
     O Jesus, my Saviour;
     He'll bring me at last to that heavenly land,
     O Jesus, my Lord.

3   I can do all things
     Through Christ my Lord who strengthens me;
     I can do all things
     Through Jesus Christ, my King!

96

When the road is rough and steep
Fix your eyes upon Jesus,
He alone has pow'r to keep,
Fix your eyes upon Him;
Jesus is a gracious friend,
One on whom you can depend,
He is faithful to the end,
Fix your eyes upon Him.

97

1 Christ be my leader
   By night as by day;
   Safe through the darkness,
   For He is the Way.
   Fears for the future
   I trust to His care;
   Darkness is daylight
   When Jesus is there.

2 Christ be my teacher
   In age as in youth,
   Drifting or doubting,
   For He is the Truth.
   Grant me to trust Him;
   Though shifting as sand,
   Doubt cannot daunt me;
   In Jesus I stand.

3 Christ be my saviour
   In calm as in strife;
   Death cannot hold me
   For He is the life.
   Nor darkness nor doubting,
   Nor sin and its stain,
   Can touch my Salvation:
   With Jesus I reign.

98

Fellows:

1 When Jesus comes to you
   He'll bring gladness, (*Girls:* gladness)
   When Jesus comes to you
   He'll bring peace; (*Girls:* He'll bring peace)
   The glory of His presence,
   From care will bring release
   When Jesus, Jesus comes to you.

   Chorus (All)

   When Jesus comes to you,
   When Jesus comes to you
   He'll fill your heart with gladness.
   You'll make others happy too;

Fellows:

2 When Jesus comes to you
   He'll bring comfort, (*Girls:* comfort)
   When Jesus comes to you
   He'll bring light; (*Girls:* He'll bring light)
   The glow of inward courage
   Will tinge the darkest night,
   When Jesus, Jesus comes to you.

   Chorus (All)

   When Jesus comes to you,
   When Jesus comes to you
   He'll fill your heart with gladness,
   When Jesus, Jesus comes to you.

99

Christ is the answer to my ev'ry need;
Christ is the answer, He is my friend indeed.
Problems of life my spirit may assail,
With Christ my Saviour I need never fail,
For Christ is the answer to my need.

100

1   When I have sorrow in my heart, what can take it
    away?
    Only Jesus in my heart can take that sorrow away.

2   When I have fear in my heart, what can take it
    away?
    Only Jesus in my heart can take that fear away.

3   When I have sin in my heart, what can take it away?
    Only Jesus in my heart can take that sin away.

4   When I have Jesus in my heart, what can take Him
    away?
    (more slowly and with emphasis)
    Once take Jesus into my heart, and He has come to
    stay.

© H. H. Lemmel and National Sunday School Union
By kind permission.

101

1   I am weak but Thou art strong;
    Jesu, keep me from all wrong;
    I'll be satisfied as long
    As I walk, let me walk, close with Thee;

        Chorus
        Just a closer walk with Thee,
        Grant it, Jesus, this my plea,
        Daily walking close with Thee,
        Let it be, dear Lord, let it be.

2   Through this world of toils and snares.
    If I falter, Lord, who cares?
    Who with me my burden shares?
    None but Thee, dear Lord, none but Thee:
        Chorus

3   When my feeble life is o'er
    Time for me will be no more,
    Guide me gently, safely home,
    To Thy Kingdom's shore, to Thy shore:
        Chorus

102

1 I do not know what lies ahead,
The way I cannot see;
Yet one stands near to be my guide,
He'll show the way to me:

> Chorus
> *I know who holds the future,*
> *And He'll guide me with His hand,*
> *With God things don't just happen,*
> *Ev'rything by Him is planned;*
> *So as I face tomorrow*
> *With its problems large and small,*
> *I'll trust the God of miracles,*
> *Give to Him my all.*

2 I do not know how many days
Of life are mine to spend;
But one who knows and cares for me
Will keep me to the end:
> *Chorus*

3 I do not know the course ahead,
What joys and griefs are there;
But one is near who fully knows,
I'll trust His loving care:
> *Chorus*

103

> Start with chorus
> *By and by when the morning comes*
> *And all the saints of God are gathering home,*
> *We will hear the story how we've overcome,*
> *And we'll understand it better by and by.*

1 Trials dark on ev'ry hand, and we cannot understand
All the ways that God will lead us
To that blessed promised land,
But He'll guide us with His eye
And we'll follow till we die,
And we'll understand it better by and by:
> *Chorus*

2 Temptations, hidden snares, often take us unawares
   And our hearts are made to bleed
   For each thoughtless word and deed;
   And we wonder why the test
   When we've tried to do our best,
   But we'll understand it better by and by:
      Chorus

104

1 Days are filled with sorrow and care,
   Hearts are lonely and drear;
   Burdens are lifted at Calvary,
   Jesus is very near.

      Chorus
      Burdens are lifted at Calvary,
      Calvary, Calvary;
      Burdens are lifted at Calvary,
      Jesus is very near.

2 Cast your care on Jesus today,
   Leave your worry and care;
   Burdens are lifted at Calvary
   Jesus is very near.
      Chorus

3 Troubled soul, the Saviour can see,
   Ev'ry heartache and tear;
   Burdens are lifted at Calvary,
   Jesus is very near.
      Chorus

105

1 Only to be what He wants me to be,
   Ev'ry moment of ev'ry day;
   Yielded completely to Jesus alone,
   Ev'ry step of this pilgrim way.

2   Just to be clay in the potter's hands,
   Ready to do what His word commands
   Only to be what He wants me to be,
   Ev'ry moment of ev'ry day.

106

Cleanse me from my sin, Lord,
Put Thy pow'r within, Lord,
Take me as I am, Lord,
And make me all Thine own;
Keep me day by day, Lord,
Underneath Thy sway, Lord,
Make my heart Thy palace
And Thy royal throne.

107

Day by day, dear Lord,
Of Thee three things I pray:
To see Thee more clearly,
To love Thee more dearly,
To follow Thee more nearly
Day by day.

108

Spirit of the Living God,
Fall afresh on me!
Spirit of the Living God,
Fall afresh on me!
Break me, melt me,
Mould me, fill me!
Spirit of the Living God,
Fall afresh on me!

109

1   They tried my Lord and Master,
    With no one to defend;
    Within the halls of Pilate
    He stood without a friend:

    Chorus

    I'll be a friend to Jesus,
    My life for Him I'll spend
    I'll be a friend to Jesus,
    Until my years shall end.

2   The world may turn against Him,
    I'll love Him to the end;
    And while on earth I'm living,
    My Lord shall have a friend:

    Chorus

3   I'll do what He may bid me,
    I'll go where He may send;
    I'll try each flying moment
    To prove that I'm His friend:

    Chorus

4   To all who need a Saviour,
    My friend I recommend;
    Because He brought salvation
    Is why I am His friend:

    Chorus

110

Start with chorus

Bring forth the fruit of the Spirit in your life
Let the life of Christ be seen in you;
Bring forth the fruit of the Spirit in your life,
And let the Lord be glorified in you.

Seek His patience and His kindness,
Seek His gentleness and self-control,
Seek His goodness and His faithfulness,
And seek most His peace, and joy, and love:

Chorus

111

1 As You cleanse me for today
And forgive my yesterday,
As you cleanse me for today
I begin anew, Lord. '

2 As You've set me in this place
And sufficient is Your grace,
As You've set me in this place
I begin anew, Lord,

3 As You're watching over me
I can face the enemy,
As You're watching over me
I begin anew, Lord.

4 As I'm ever in Your sight
In the depth or in the height,
As I'm ever in Your sight
I begin anew, Lord.

112

1 O Holy Spirit, giver of life,
You bring our souls immortality;
Yet in our hearts is struggle and strife,
We need your inward vitality;
Work out within us the Father's design,
Give to us life, O Spirit Divine.

2   O Holy Spirit, giver of light,
     To minds where all is obscurity;
     Exchange for blindness, spiritual sight,
     That we may grow to maturity;
     Work out within us the Father's design,
     Give to us light, O Spirit Divine.

3   O Holy Spirit, giver of love,
     And joy, and peace, and fidelity;
     The fruitfulness which comes from above,
     That self-control and humility;
     Work out within us the Father's design,
     Give to us love, O Spirit Divine.

113

1   There is a place of quiet rest,
     Near to the heart of God,
     A place where sin cannot molest,
     Near to the heart of God.

          Chorus

          O Jesus, blest Redeemer,
          Sent from the heart of God,
          Hold us, who wait before Thee,
          Near to the heart of God.

2   There is a place of comfort sweet,
     Near to the heart of God,
     A place where we our Saviour meet,
     Near to the heart of God.
          Chorus

3   There is a place of full release,
     Near to the heart of God,
     A place where all is joy and peace,
     Near to the heart of God:
          Chorus

114

According to the working of His mighty pow'r
We are raised up together with Christ.
According to the pleasure of His holy will
We are sanctified.
According to the riches of His glory and His grace
He supplies our ev'ry need,
So that henceforth we might live only unto Him,
Our friend and Lord indeed.

115

Lord, make me useful to Thee,
Send now Thy Spirit to me,
Thy perfect will
In me fulfil,
Lord, make me useful to Thee.

116

1   His hands were pierced, the hands that made
    The mountain range and everglade;
    That washed the stains of sin away
    And changed earth's darkness into day.

2   His feet were pierced, the feet that trod
    The furthest shining star of God;
    And left their imprint deep and clear
    On ev'ry winding pathway here.

3   His heart was pierced, the heart that burned
    To comfort ev'ry heart that yearned;
    And from it came a cleansing flood,
    The river of redeeming blood.

4   His hands and feet and heart, all three
    Were pierced for me on Calvary;
    And here and now, to Him I bring,
    My hands, feet, heart, an offering.

117

1   Though days are long, oft filled with care,
    Though burdens seem so hard to bear
    No matter what my lot may be,
    I'll live for Him who died for me:

        Chorus

        I'll live for Jesus day after day,
        I'll live for Jesus let come what may,
        The Holy Spirit I will obey,
        And live for Jesus day after day.

2   Through ev'ry day new joy I find.
    He gives to me real peace of mind,
    Until the day when Christ I'll see,
    I'll live for Him who died for me:
        Chorus

© Fiesta Music Inc. 1954, Box 2471, Hollywood 28, California, U.S.A. *By kind permission*

118

1   Creator God, Creator God!
    With Thee I am a man,
    But without Thee, O Lord my Saviour,
    Without Thee I am just a child.

2   Creator God, Creator God!
    With Thy hands may I work,
    With Thy feet may I walk, O Saviour,
    And through Thine own eyes let me see.

3   And with Thy heart, Creator God,
    I will learn and love,
    With Thy heart, O Creator God
    I'll learn and love like Thee.

119

I'll live for Christ who gave Himself on the tree,
I'm crucified with Christ whose death set me free,
And yet I live, for Christ is living in me:

I'll live for Christ alway,
I'll live for Christ alway,
I'll serve Him ev'ry day;
I'll live by faith in Christ and trust in His grace;
I'll live for Christ alway.

© M. A. Baughen
By kind permission

120

Version 1

Give me oil in my lamp, keep me burning,
Give me oil in my lamp, I pray;
Give me oil in my lamp, keep me burning,
Keep me burning 'til the break of day:

Chorus

Sing Hosanna! Sing Hosanna!
Sing Hosanna to the King of Kings!
Sing Hosanna! Sing Hosanna!
Sing Hosanna to the King.

(**N.B.** 2 *part chorus – One group sustain 'Sing'*
while the other group does 'Sing Hosanna', etc.)

Version 2

1 Give me joy in my heart, keep me praising,
   Give me joy in my heart, I pray;
   Give me joy in my heart, keep me praising,
   Keep me praising 'til the break of day:
   Chorus as version 1

2 Give me peace in my heart, keep me resting . . .
   Chorus

3 Give me love in my heart, keep me serving . . .
   Chorus

Version 3

1. What a wonderful Saviour is Jesus,
   What a wonderful friend is He,
   For He left all the glory of heaven,
   Came to earth to die on Calvary:
      Chorus as version 1

2. He arose from the grave, Hallelujah.
   And He lives never more to die,
   At the Father's right hand interceding,
   He will hear and heed our faintest cry:
      Chorus

3. He is coming some day to receive us,
   We'll be caught up to heaven above,
   What a joy it will be to behold Him,
   Sing forever of His grace and love:
      Chorus

121

1. I want to walk with Jesus Christ,
   All the days I live of this life on earth,
   To give to Him complete control
   Of body and of soul:

   Chorus
   Follow Him, follow Him, yield your life to Him,
   He has conquered death, He is King of Kings,
   Accept the joy which He gives to those
   Who yield their lives to Him.

2. I want to learn to speak to Him,
   To pray to Him, confess my sin,
   To open my life and let Him in,
   For joy will then be mine:
      Chorus

3 I want to learn to speak of Him,
   My life must show that He lives in me,
   My deeds, my thoughts, my words must speak
   All of His love for me:
      Chorus

4 I want to learn to read His Word,
   For this is how I know the way
   To live my life as pleases Him,
   In holiness and joy:
      Chorus

5 O Holy Spirit of the Lord,
   Enter now into this heart of mine,
   Take full control of my selfish will
   And make me wholly Thine:
      Chorus

122

1 O when you come to the end of life's journey,
   Weary and worn, and the battle is done,
   Carrying the Cross, the Cross of redemption,
   He'll understand and say 'Well done',
   He'll understand and say 'Well done'.

2 Give, when you give, the best of your service,
   Telling the world that the Saviour has come;
   Be not dismayed if men won't defend you,
   He'll understand and say 'Well done',
   He'll understand and say 'Well done'.

3 O when you try, and fail in your trying,
   Hands sore and scarred from the work you have
      begun,
   Come to the cross, come quickly to Jesus,
   He'll understand and say 'Well done',
   He'll understand and say 'Well done'.

123

1 Looking unto Jesus
Who has gone before,
Now enthroned in glory,
King for evermore.
Born again of His Spirit,
Saved by His shed blood,
Given work to be done for Him,
Joined to Him by love:

> Chorus
> *Looking unto Jesus*
> *Who has gone before,*
> *Now enthroned in glory,*
> *King for evermore.*

2 Looking unto Jesus,
In the Christian fight,
Seeking grace to witness,
Strengthened by His might,
With the armour of Jesus,
With the Spirit's sword,
With much prayer that He'll bless His Word,
Fighting for the Lord:
> *Chorus*

3 Looking unto Jesus
Who despised the shame,
Throwing off all hindrance
As we bear His Name.
Help us face all temptation,
Lord, help us discern,
Give us courage to speak for Thee
Help our light to burn:
> *Chorus*

© M. A. Baughen 1964 *By kind permission*

124

O Jesus, Lord and Saviour, I give myself to Thee;
For Thou, in Thy atonement, didst give Thyself for
  me;
I own no other master, my heart shall be Thy throne;
My life I give, henceforth to live, O Christ, for Thee
  alone.

125

1 I have decided to follow Jesus,
 I have decided to follow Jesus,
 I have decided to follow Jesus,
 No turning back, no turning back.

2 The cross before me, the world behind me,
 The cross before me, the world behind me,
 The cross before me, the world behind me,
 No turning back, no turning back.

126

1 Lord Jesus Christ,
 You have come to us,
 You are one with us,
 Mary's Son.
 Cleansing our souls from all their sin,
 Pouring Your love and goodness in,
 Jesus, our love for You we sing,
 Living Lord.

At Communion
2 Lord Jesus Christ,
 Now and every day,
 Teach us how to pray,
 Son of God,
 You have commanded us to do
 This in remembrance, Lord, of You:
 Into our lives Your power breaks through,
 Living Lord.

3 Lord Jesus Christ,
 You have come to us,
 Born as one of us,
 Mary's Son.
 Led out to die on Calvary,
 Risen from death to set us free,
 Living Lord Jesus, help us see
 You are Lord.

4 Lord Jesus Christ,
  I would come to You,
  Live my life for You,
  Son of God.
  All Your commands I know are true,
  Your many gifts will make me new,
  Into my life Your power breaks through,
  Living Lord.

127

1 To Him we come:
  Jesus Christ our Lord,
  God's own living Word,
  His dear Son.
  In Him there is no east and west,
  In Him all nations shall be blest;
  To all He offers peace and rest,
  Loving Lord.

2 In Him we live:
  Christ our strength and stay,
  Life, and Truth, and Way,
  Friend divine.
  His power can break the chains of sin,
  Still all life's storms without, within,
  Help us the daily fight to win,
  Living Lord.

3 For Him we go:
  Soldiers of the cross,
  Counting all things loss,
  Him to know;
  Going to men of every race,
  Preaching to all His wondrous grace,
  Building His Church in every place,
  Conquering Lord.

4 With Him we serve:
  His the work we share
  With saints everywhere,
  Near and far;

One in the task which faith requires,
One in the zeal which never tires,
One in the hope His love inspires,
Coming Lord.

5 Onward we go,
Faithful, bold, and true,
His blest will to do,
Day by day.
Till, at the last, with joy, we'll see
Jesus, in glorious majesty;
Live with Him through eternity,
Reigning Lord!

128

Ev'ry person in ev'ry nation
In each succeeding generation
Has the right to hear the news
That Christ can save.

Crucified on Calv'ry's mountain
He opened wide a cleansing fountain,
Conquered sin and death and hell,
He rose up from the grave.

Father, I am willing to dedicate to Thee
Life and talent, time and money:
Here am I, send me.

129

1 A vessel called the Church of God
Sails over time's great sea;
She sets her course for God's great port
To God's eternity.
    The world attacks her like a storm
    There's danger, need, and fear;
    She sails with hope and victory
    Through ev'ry passing year.

The question constantly is asked,
Can this great ship endure?
Can she survive the world's attacks?
Is victory secure?

Chorus
We can triumph, Lord,
As You stay with us, Lord,
We will sail on the turbulent sea of this life
And sail with You as Lord!

2   What happens if the ship remains
At moorings by the quay?
What happens if she wants the calm
And will not put to sea?
     It may be nice to glory in
     The vict'ries of the past,
     But God wants us to sail today –
     His colours at the mast!
The course of God is sacrifice,
We must not fear the cost;
The life not lived for Christ the Lord
Is life which God calls lost:
     Chorus

3   The ship we call the Church of God
Depends upon its crew;
There are no passengers aboard,
There's work for all to do.
     God has a post for ev'ryone,
     A duty to fulfil;
     He gifted us, now looks to us,
     To do His perfect will.
We work together as a team
With fellowship in Him,
We have a common faith and hope –
The Spirit's power within:
     Chorus

4   The ship has many would-be guides
Who state what course they think;
They rest upon man's thought alone
And with them we would sink!

But God has made His course quite clear,
His way is in His Word;
We see the fulness of the truth
As we look to the Lord.
When onslaughts come upon our faith
Let courage flood our hearts;
We are a world-wide fellowship
And share all God imparts:
    Chorus

130

1 There's a road which leads from Jerusalem,
    It's the way down to Jericho,
    It's Compassion road, steep and tiring road,
    Which has danger from thieving foe.
    And here on this road is one man
    Beaten up and left as half dead,
    Like many in this world around us
    Oppressed, in despair or unfed.
    Hear him cry out
    As he lies on Compassion road.

2 Watch a priest and Levite come down that road
    Only giving the man small heed,
    They are too caught up with religious thoughts
    To give help to a man in need.
    Samaritan, walk behind them!
    You are not within the same class!
    But you are the one who helps him –
    You could not see need and just pass!
    You heard the cry
    As you walked on Compassion road.

3 The Compassion road goes right on through life,
    It's a road with us still today,
    Many hands are needed to give the help
    To those stricken upon the way.
    So now will you have compassion?

To the lonely, hungry, and worn,
To those without hope or salvation,
To fearful and poor and forlorn?
Lord, give us grace
To give help on Compassion road.

131

1 The fields are white unto harvest time,
Look up and see!
The fields are white unto harvest time,
Look up and see:

> Chorus
> *Pray to the Lord of the harvest,*
> *Christ says pray.*
> *Pray to the Lord for the workers*
> *Which we need in this day.*

2 The harvest truly is fit to reap
But workers few,
The harvest truly is fit to reap
But workers few:
> *Chorus*

3 Who else will 'go into all the world'
To preach the Word?
Who else will 'go into all the world'
To preach the Word?
> *Chorus*

4 The Lord's return may be very soon,
The time is short!
The Lord's return may be very soon,
The time is short:
> *Chorus*

132

1 Go forth and tell! O Church of God, awake!
God's saving news to all the nations take.
Proclaim Christ Jesus, Saviour Lord, and King,
That all the world His worthy praise may sing.

2   Go forth and tell! God's love embraces all:
     He will in grace respond to all who call.
     How shall they call if they have never heard
     The gracious invitation of His Word?

3   Go forth and tell! Men still in darkness lie:
     In wealth or want, in sin they live and die.
     Give us, O Lord, concern of heart and mind,
     A love like Thine which cares for all mankind.

4   Go forth and tell! The doors are open wide:
     Share God's good gifts with men so long denied.
     Live out your life as Christ, your Lord, shall choose,
     Your ransomed powers for His sole glory use.

5   Go forth and tell! O Church of God, arise:
     Go in the strength which Christ your Lord supplies.
     Go, till all nations His great Name adore
     And serve Him Lord and King for evermore.

© J. E. Seddon 1964 *By kind permission*

133

1   O when the saints go marching in,
     O when the saints go marching in;
     O Lord, I want to be among the number
     When the saints go marching in.

2   O when they crown Him Lord of all,
     O when they crown Him Lord of all;
     O Lord, I want to be among the number
     When they crown Him Lord of all.

3   O when all knees bow at His name,
     O when all knees bow at His name;
     O Lord, I want to be among the number
     When all knees bow at His name.

4   O when they sing the Saviour's praise,
     O when they sing the Saviour's praise;
     O Lord, I want to be among the number
     When they sing the Saviour's praise.

5 O when the saints go marching in,
   O when the saints go marching in;
   O Lord, I want to be among the number
   When the saints go marching in.

134

1 I gotta home in gloryland that outshines the sun,
   I gotta home in gloryland that outshines the sun,
   I gotta home in gloryland that outshines the sun,
   Way beyond the blue:

   Chorus
   Do Lord, oh, do Lord, oh, do remember me;
   Do Lord, oh, do Lord, oh, do remember me;
   Do Lord, oh, do Lord, oh, do remember me;
   Way beyond the blue.

2 I took Jesus as my Saviour,
   you take Him too . . .

3 If you will not bear a cross,
   you can't wear a crown . . .

Alternative version
1 I gotta home in gloryland that outshines the sun,
   I gotta home in gloryland that outshines the sun,
   I gotta home in gloryland that outshines the sun,
   Way beyond the blue:

   Chorus
   Thank You, my Saviour, for that eternal life;
   Thank You, my Saviour, for that eternal life;
   Thank You, my Saviour, for that eternal life
   With You evermore!

2 Those who trust in Christ as Saviour,
   shall never die . . .

3 If you will not bear a cross,
   you can't wear a crown . . .

135

1   When I come to the river at ending of day
    When the last winds of sorrow have blown,
    There'll be somebody waiting to show me the way,
    I won't have to cross Jordan alone:

    Chorus
    I won't have to cross Jordan alone,
    Jesus died for my sins to atone;

    (solo) When the darkness I see, He'll be waiting
        for me,
    I won't have to cross Jordan alone.

2   Oftentimes I'm forsaken, and weary and sad
    When it seems that my friends have all gone,
    There is one thought that cheers me and makes my
        heart glad
    I won't have to cross Jordan alone:
        Chorus

3   Though the billows of sorrow and trouble may
        sweep,
    Christ the Saviour will care for His own;
    Till the end of the journey, my soul He will keep,
    I won't have to cross Jordan alone:
        Chorus

136

1   This world is not my home,
    I'm just a-passing through;
    My treasures are laid up
    Somewhere beyond the blue;
    The Saviour beckons me
    From heaven's open door,
    And I can't feel at home
    In this world any more.

Chorus
O Lord, you know, I have no friend like you;
If heaven's not my home, then Lord what will I do?
The Saviour beckons me from heaven's open door,
And I can't feel at home in this world any more.

2 They're all expecting me,
And that's one thing I know,
My Saviour pardoned me,
Now onward I must go;
I know He'll take me through
Though I am weak and poor,
And I can't feel at home
In this world any more.
    Chorus

3 Just over in glory land
We'll live eternally,
The saints on every hand
Are shouting victory;
Their songs of sweetest praise
Drift back from heaven's shore,
And I can't feel at home
In this world any more.
    Chorus

137

Start with Chorus
O sinner man, where will you run to?
O sinner man, where will you run to?
O sinner man, where will you run to
All on that day?

1 Run to the rocks, rocks won't you hide me?
Run to the rocks, rocks won't you hide me?
Run to the rocks, rocks won't you hide me,
All on that day?
    Chorus

2 Run to the sea, sea is a-boiling,
  Run to the sea, sea is a-boiling,
  Run to the sea, sea is a-boiling,
  All on that day.
    Chorus

3 Run to the Lord, Lord won't you hide me?
  Run to the Lord, Lord won't you hide me?
  Run to the Lord, Lord won't you hide me,
  All on that day.
    Chorus

4 O sinner man, should bin a-praying,
  O sinner man, should bin a-praying,
  O sinner man, should bin a-praying,
  All on that day.
    Chorus

138

(*solo*)
1 If religion were a thing
    (*Everyone else*) *If religion were a thing*
  That money could buy,
                That money could buy
  Then the rich would live
                Then the rich would live
  And the poor would die:
                And the poor would die

  Chorus
  All my sins be taken away,
  All glory be to His Name,
  All my sins be taken away,
  Be taken away,

2 Christ died for us all, He died upon the tree,
  But now He lives, He lives in me:
    Chorus

3 We praise Thee, O God, we acknowledge Thee
  To be the Lord, the Lord most high:
    Chorus

Alternative version

1 Our Father which art in heaven,
   Hallowed be Thy Name; Thy kingdom come.
      Chorus

2 Thy will be done in earth as in heaven,
   Put us not to the test, lead us not into wrong.
      Chorus

139

1 You've got to walk that lonesome valley,
   You've got to walk there by yourself;
   And no one here can walk there for you,
   You've got to walk there by yourself.

2 You've got to face one day your Maker,
   You've got to face Him by yourself;
   And no one here can face Him for you,
   You've got to face Him by yourself.

3 You've got to stand one day in Judgment,
   You've got to stand there by yourself;
   And no one here can stand there for you,
   You've got to stand there by yourself.

4 You've got to walk that lonesome valley,
   You've got to walk there by yourself;
   And no one here can walk there for you,
   You've got to walk there by yourself.

140

1 Where you there when they crucified my Lord?
   Where you there when they crucified my Lord?
   Oh! Sometimes it causes me to tremble, tremble,
      tremble.
   Were you there when they crucified my Lord?

2 Were you there when they nailed Him to the tree?

3   Were you there when they pierced Him in the side?

4   Were you there when the sun refused to shine?

5   Were you there when they laid Him in the tomb?

6   Were you there when He rose up from the dead?
     Were you there when He rose up from the dead?
     O-o-oh! Sometimes I feel like shouting glory, glory,
         glory!
     Were you there when He rose up from the dead?

141

1   Steal away, steal away,
     Steal away to Jesus;
     Steal away, steal away home,
     I ain't got long to stay here.

         Chorus
         My Lord He calls me;
         He calls me by the thunder;
         The trumpet sounds within my soul.
         I ain't got long to stay here.

2   Green trees are bending,
     The sinner stands a-trembling;
     The trumpet sounds within my soul;
     I ain't got long to stay here.
         Chorus

3   My Lord He calls me;
     He calls me by the lightning;
     The trumpet sounds within my soul;
     I ain't got long to stay here:
         Chorus

142

Start with chorus
Is there anybody here who loves my Jesus?
Anybody here who loves my Lord?
I want to know, yes, I want to know,
Do you love my Lord?

1   I want to sing that I love my Jesus;
    I want to shout that I love my Lord:
    I want to know, yes, I want to know,
    Do you love my Lord?
         Chorus

2   Makes us feel like shouting when you love my
         Jesus;
    Makes us feel like shouting when you love my
         Lord:
    I want to know, yes, I want to know,
    Do you love my Lord?
         Chorus

3   Shout it from the mountains if you love my Jesus;
    Sing it in the valleys if you love my Lord:
    I want to know, yes, I want to know,
    Do you love my Lord?
         Chorus

143

N.B. Some sing as the chorus:
Little David followed the Lord,
Why don't you? Why don't you?

Start with chorus
Little David, play on your harp,
Hallelu, Hallelu,
Little David, play on your harp,
Hallelu.

1   Little David was a shepherd boy;
    He killed Goliath, shouted for joy:
         Chorus

2   Joshua was the son of Nun,
    He never would quit till the work was done:
       Chorus

144

1   The gospel train's a-coming, I hear it close at hand
    I hear those car wheels rumbling and moving
    through the land:

    Chorus
    Get on board, little children, get on board,
    Little children, get on board, little children,
    There's room for many'a more.

2   I hear the bell and whistle, a-coming round the
    curve,
    She's playing all the steam and power, and straining
    every nerve:
       Chorus

3   The fare is cheap and all can go, the rich and poor
    are there,
    No second class aboard that train, no difference in
    the fare:
       Chorus

4   No signal for another train to follow on the line,
    O sinner, you're for ever lost if once you're left
    behind:
       Chorus

5   She's nearing now the station – O sinner, don't be
    vain;
    O come and get your ticket, and be ready for that
    train:
       Chorus

145

1 Lord, I want to be a Christian in my heart, in my
   heart,
   Lord, I want to be a Christian in my heart,
   In my heart, in my heart,
   Lord I want to be a Christian in my heart.

2 Lord, I want to be more loving in my heart . . .

3 Lord, I want to be more holy in my heart . . .

4 Lord, I want to be like Jesus in my heart . . .

146

Start with chorus
Joshua fought the battle of Jericho,
Jericho, Jericho,
Joshua fought the battle of Jericho,
And the walls came a-tumbling down.

1 You may talk of your King of Gibeon,
  You may talk of your man of Saul,
  There's none like good old Joshua.
  And the battle of Jericho:
     Chorus

2 Up to the walls of Jericho
  He marched with spear in hand,
  'Go blow them rams horns', Joshua cried,
  'For the battle is in my hand.'
     Chorus

3 Then the lam rams sheephorns begin to blow,
  Trumpets began to sound;
  Joshua commanded the people to shout,
  And the walls came a-tumbling down:
     Chorus

147

1 Goin' to lay down my burden
   Down by the riverside,
   Down by the riverside,
   Down by the riverside;
   Goin' to lay down my burden
   Down by the riverside,
   And grieve my Lord no more:

     Chorus
     Ain't goin' to grieve my Lord no more,
     Ain't goin' to grieve my Lord no more,
     Ain't goin' to grieve my Lord no more,
     Ain't goin' to grieve my Lord no more,
     Ain't goin' to grieve my Lord no more,
     Ain't goin' to grieve my Lord no more.

2 Goin' to lay down my sword and shield . . .
3 Goin' to try on my long white robe . . .
4 Goin' to try on my starry crown . . .

   Alternative version

1 Goin' to lay down my burden . . .
2 Goin' to sing for my Saviour . . .
3 Goin' to talk to my Maker . . .
4 Goin' to follow my Master . . .

148

1 Somebody's knocking at your door,
   Somebody's knocking at your door;
   O sinner, why don't you answer?
   Somebody's knocking at your door.

2 Knocks like Jesus,
   Somebody's knocking at your door:
   Knocks like Jesus,
   Somebody's knocking at your door.
   O sinner, why don't you answer?
   Somebody's knocking at your door.

3   Can't you hear Him?
    Somebody's knocking at your door;
    Can't you hear Him?
    Somebody's knocking at your door.
    O sinner, why don't you answer?
    Somebody's knocking at your door.

4   Answer Jesus,
    Somebody's knocking at your door;
    Answer Jesus,
    Somebody's knocking at your door.
    O sinner, why don't you answer?
    Somebody's knocking at your door.

149

Start with chorus
There is a balm in Gilead
To make the wounded whole,
There is a balm in Gilead
To heal the sin-sick soul.

1   Sometimes I feel discouraged
    And think my work's in vain,
    But then the Holy Spirit
    Revives my soul again:
        Chorus

2   You cannot sing like angels,
    You cannot preach like Paul,
    But you can tell of Jesus
    And say He died for all:
        Chorus

150

Start with chorus
Go tell it on the mountain
Over the hills and ev'rywhere;
Go tell it on the mountain
That Jesus Christ is Lord.

1   Oh, when I was a seeker
    I sought both night and day;
    I asked the Lord to help me,
    And He showed me the way:
        Chorus

2   He made me a watchman,
    Upon the city wall;
    To tell of His salvation
    For Jesus died for all:
        Chorus

3   Go tell it to your neighbour
    In darkness here below;
    Go with the words of Jesus,
    That all the world may know:
        Chorus

YOUTH PRAISE 2

151

Let us praise,
As we raise
Heart and voice to God above.
Let it ring,
As we sing
Out the story of His love.
Let it flow,
Let it grow,
Let it rise from ev'ry shore:
Be adored,
Christ the Lord,
Praise His Name for evermore!
© G. Brattle 1969   *By kind permission*

152

1 Let us praise God together,
   Let us praise.
   Let us praise God together,
   Him proclaim.
      He is faithful in all His ways,
      He is worthy of all our praise,
      His Name be exalted on high.

2 Let us seek God together,
   Let us pray,
   Let us seek His forgiveness
   As we pray.
      He will cleanse us from all sin,
      He will help us the fight to win,
      His Name be exalted on high.

3 Let us serve God together,
   Let us serve;
   Let our lives show His goodness
   As we work.
      Christ the Lord is the world's true light,
      Let us serve Him with all our might;
      His Name be exalted on high.
© J. E. Seddon 1969   *By kind permission*

153

Blessed be the Lord who daily bears us up,
He takes our cares.
Blessed be the Lord.
Even the God of our salvation.
Blessed be the Lord.
Blessed be the Lord.

154

1 I've got something now to sing about,
  and shout about,
  and tell around.
 I've got ev'rything to sing about,
  since Jesus took my sins away.
   I know that Jesus, He is my Saviour;
    oh, how He suffered for me.
   God's judgment poured on Him my
    Lord and He did it for me,
  So that I could be free.

2 I've got something now to sing about,
  and shout about,
  and tell around.
 Life for me is now so wonderful,
  since Jesus took my sins away.
   Each day now ev'rywhere that I go
   I know Jesus is there by my side.
   His life within helps me to win over
    anger and pride, 'cos He's living inside.

3 I've got ev'rything to sing about,
  and shout about,
  and tell around.
 Oh just let me tell to ev'ryone, how Jesus
  died and rose again.
   Right down into this sin-sick world,
    from Heaven's glory He came.
   To bleed and die on Calvary's cross to
    save us from sin and shame, He came.

4   I've got ev'rything to sing about,
        and shout about,
        and tell around.
    Oh just let me tell to ev'ryone, how Jesus
        died and rose again.
            Each day now ev'rywhere that I go I know
                Jesus is there by my side
                His life within helps me to win over
                    anger and pride, 'cos He's living inside.

    I've got ev'rything to sing about,
        and shout about,
        and tell around.
    Life for me is now so wonderful,
        since Jesus took my sins away.
    Life for me is now so wonderful, since
        Jesus took my sins away.

155

1   There is joy, there is joy,
    There is joy before the angels over
    Every person who repents of sin.
    There is joy, there is joy,
    There is joy before the angels over
    Every sinner who repents.

        All the heavens ring
        As the angels sing,
        And worship our most glorious King.
        And they praise the name
        Of the Lord who came
        To seek the blind and lost and lame.

2   There is joy, there is joy,
    There is joy before the angels over
    Every person who repents of sin.
    There is joy, there is joy,
    There is joy before the angels over
    Every sinner who repents.

156

1 Lord, for the years Your love has kept and
      guided,
   Urged and inspired us, cheered us on our way,
   Sought us and saved us, pardoned and provided.
   Lord of the years, we bring our thanks today.

2 Lord, for that Word, the Word of life which
      fires us,
   Speaks to our hearts and sets our souls ablaze,
   Teaches and trains, rebukes us and inspires us,
   Lord of the Word, receive Your people's praise.

3 Lord, for our land, in this our generation,
   Spirits oppressed by pleasure, wealth and care;
   For young and old, for commonwealth and
      nation,
   Lord of our land, be pleased to hear our prayer.

4 Lord, for our world, when men disown and
      doubt Him,
   Loveless in strength, and comfortless in pain;
   Hungry and helpless, lost indeed without Him,
   Lord of the world, we pray that Christ may
      reign.

5 Lord for ourselves; in living power remake us—
   Self on the cross and Christ upon the throne—
   Past put behind us, for the future take us,
   Lord of our lives, to live for Christ alone.
   © T. Dudley-Smith 1967 *By kind permission*

157

1 Sing praise to God who reigns above,
   The God of all creation,
   The God of power, the God of love,
   The God of our salvation;
   With healing balm my soul He fills,
   And every faithless murmur stills:
   To God all praise and glory.

2 What God's almighty power hath made,
  His gracious mercy keepeth;
  By morning glow or evening shade
  His watchful eye ne'er sleepeth;
  Within the kingdom of his might,
  Lo! all is just and all is right:
  To God all praise and glory.

3 The Lord is never far away,
  But, through all grief distressing,
  An ever-present help and stay,
  Our peace, and joy, and blessing;
  As with a mother's tender hand,
  He leads His own, His chosen band:
  To God all praise and glory.

4 Thus, all my toilsome way along,
  I sing aloud Thy praises,
  That men may hear the grateful song
  My voice unwearied raises;
  Be joyful in the Lord, my heart,
  Both soul and body bear your part:
  To God all praise and glory.

158

Be this my joy today,
To hear and to obey
My Saviours' word, His wonderful word.
To read in ev'ry line
God's will, and make it mine—
Be this my joy, my wonderful joy!
© G. Brattle   *By kind permission*

159

Start with Chorus
In my heart there sings a song,
Song of all eternity,
In my heart there sings a song
Of my Saviour's love to me.

1 He for me left behind the Father's throne—
  For me, just a sinner like me.
  And for me He was left all alone—
  For me, yes dear Lord, just for me.
  Chorus

2 He for me came to be crucified—
   For me, just a sinner like me.
   And for me came to suffer and die—
   For me, yes dear Lord, just for me.
       Chorus

3 He for me rose again from the grave—
   For me, just a sinner like me.
   And for me He will come back one day—
   For me, yes dear Lord, just for me.
       Chorus

© Charles Roda *By kind permission*

160

1 Blessed is the man—the man who does not walk
   In the counsel of the wicked—blessed is
       that man.
   He who rejects the way—rejects the way of sin
   And who turns away from scoffing—blessed
       is that man.
   But his delight by day and night
   Is the law of God Almighty.

2 He is like a tree—a tree that flourishes
   Being planted by the water—blessed is that man.
   He will bring forth fruit—his leaf will
       wither not—
   For in all he does he prospers—blessed is
       that man.
   For his delight—by day and night—
   Is the law of God Almighty.

3 The wicked are not so—for they are like the
       chaff—
   Which the wind blows clean away—the wicked
       are not so.
   The wicked will not stand—on the judgment
       day—
   Nor belong to God's people—the wicked will
       not stand.
   But God knows the way of righteous men
   And ungodly ways will perish.

Blessed is the man, the man who does
    not walk
In the counsel of the wicked—blessed is
    that man.

161

1   Why do the heathen conspire?
    Peoples are plotting in vain,
    Kings of the earth declare
    Against God and His Anointed One:
        'Break all their bonds asunder,
        Let us be done with their cords.'

2   He who is sitting in heaven
    Laughs them to scorn, as the Lord,
    He will address them in wrath
    And they fear as they listen to His words:
        'I have set up my true King,
        He is on my holy hill.'

3   This is the word from the Lord—
    He told me, 'You are my son:
    Ask of me and I will make
    All the nations of earth your heritage.
        You shall bruise them with iron
        Dash them in pieces like a vase.'

4   Now therefore, kings of the earth,
    Think and take warning from this.
    Yield to the Lord and serve Him
    Kneeling down before Him in reverence.
        Do not ignore and perish—
        Blessed are all those who trust in Him.

162

Start with chorus
O Lord, Our God!
How majestic is Your name in all the earth!

1   Your glory is transcendent
    Yet children sing Your praise
    Your enemies are silenced
    Before Your majesty.
        Chorus

2 I stand to view the heavens
  Created by Your hands
  You placed the moon and stars there
  And yet You care for man.
    Chorus

3 To man You gave such honour
  You made him almost god
  In giving him dominion
  Over created things.
    Chorus

4 You put beneath man's ruling
  All animals of earth
  The birds that fly above him
  And all within the sea.
    O Lord, Our God!
    How majestic is Your name in all the earth!
    O Lord, Our God!
    How majestic is Your name in all the earth!

© M. A. Baughen 1969   *By kind permission*

163

1 O Lord, our Lord, how majestic Thy name is,
  How great is Thy name in all the earth
  Who hast set Thy glory above the high heavens
  And stilleth Thy foes through a child in
    its birth.

2 When I think of Thy heavens, the work of
    Thy fingers,
  The moon and the stars which Thou
    hast ordained
  What is man in Thy mem'ry, a man that
    Thou mindest,
  The son of man that Thou carest for him.

3 Thou hast made him just lower than angels
    of glory
  And crowned him with honour and glory and
    power
  Thou gavest dominion o'er all of the wide earth,
  And all of the creatures that run in the sea.

© Ewald Bash   *By kind permission*

164

1. The Lord is my Shepherd, I never shall want;
   He makes me in pastures to lie;
   Beside the still waters He gently will lead,
   My needs He will daily supply.

2. The Lord is my Saviour, my soul He restores,
   He found me when lost and astray;
   He shows me the way of His Truth and
   His will,
   And helps me to trust and obey.

3. The Lord is my shield, I no evil shall fear;
   He lightens the dark paths I tread;
   He always is with me, my rod and my staff,
   And now death itself has no dread.

4. The Lord is my strength, at His table I find
   The pow'r to defeat all my foes;
   My life He sustains with His kindness and
   power,
   With blessings my cup overflows.

5. The Lord is my song, of His grace I will sing,
   I'll dwell in His house all my days;
   His goodness and mercy will follow me still,
   His Name I for ever will praise.
   © J. E. Seddon 1969 *By kind permission*

165

1. The earth is the Lord's and the fulness thereof,
   The world and the people therein.
   He has founded it upon the seas,
   On river floods He established all things.

2. So who shall ascend on the hill of the Lord?
   Or stand in the holiest place?
   He whose hands are clean and heart is pure,
   Who is not false and is not deceitful.

3. And he will receive all the blessing of God
   His Saviour will vindicate him.
   Such is everyone who seeks the Lord,
   Who seeks the face of the God of Jacob.

4 Now lift up your heads O you gates and you
    doors
  The King of all Glory comes in!
  Who then is this King of Glory—who?
  The Lord Himself who is strong and mighty.

5 Now lift up your heads O you gates and you
    doors,
  The King of all Glory comes in!
  Who then is this King of Glory—who?
  The Lord of Hosts is the King of Glory!

166

1 The Lord is my light and salvation in life
  The Lord is my stronghold, so whom shall I
    fear?
    Though men may assail me
    They will stumble and fall
  For though battles rage, I will trust in the Lord

2 One thing which I seek is to live in God's hous
  To gaze on His beauty and learn more of Him
    In trouble He will protect me
    Lifting my head
  And I will rejoice and will sing to the Lord!

3 O Lord hear my voice when I call upon You,
  You said 'Seek my face' and Your face do I
    seek.
    In anger do not reject me
    You are my help
  I know I will see all Your goodness, O Lord!

167

1 I waited patiently for the Lord
  He turned and listened to me
  He drew me out of the echoing pit
  And out of the miry clay.
  He set my feet upon a rock
  My footsteps He made secure
  Within my mouth He put a new song
  A song of praise to God.

2 In many seeing it, fear will come—
They then will turn to the Lord
And he is happy who trusts in the Lord
Who will not be led astray.
Your wondrous deeds and thoughts to us
Are multiplied, O my God—
They number more than we can proclaim
Lord! None compares with You!

3 It is not offerings You require
But open ears to Your word
And so instead of a sacrifice
I come to you with my life.
I love to do Your will, my God,
Within my heart is Your law;
Deliverance is news I have told—
My lips have not been sealed.

4 I have not hidden within my heart
Your steadfast love and Your help—
The congregation has heard me declare
Salvation and faithfulness.
And so when evils circle me
Have mercy on me, O Lord
May all who love You thankfully say:
The Lord is great indeed!

© M. A. Baughen 1969   *By kind permission*

168

1 Have mercy, Lord, as You promise,
Wash me and cleanse me from my guilt,
For I can see the wrong in my life,
Against You, Lord, have I sinned.

2 In judgment, Your word is blameless,
For I have sinned since my beginning,
And Lord, You long for truth in my life,
So give me wisdom today.

3 Lord, wash me from my uncleanness,
Fill me with joy where once was sadness,
Give me a heart renewed, O my Lord,
A new right spirit within.

4   Turn from my sins and destroy them,
    But let me never be forsaken.
    O give me joy in knowing You save,
    And make me love Your command.

5   I'll tell all those who ignore You
    And sinners then will come repentant.
    Lord, save me from the death I deserve
    Then I will tell what You've done.

6   Lord take my lips and I'll praise You;
    No sacrifice I bring redeems me.
    All that You want is my broken heart;
    A gift You will not refuse.

7   Lord give Your peace to Your servant.
    Protect and stay by me for ever.
    Through Your great love accept what I give
    And fill my life with Your praise.

169

1   If the building is not of the Lord,
    There's no use in starting the building.
    If the Lord is not watching the town,
    There's no point in having it guarded.

      Chorus
      Praise Him in whom we can trust
      Jesus our rock, our strong defence.
      Praise Him for life that's secure,
      For love that will not end.

2   You're careful to wake with the dawn.
    For your wages you toil till the evening.
    But the Lord gives the ones that He loves
    All His gifts even while they are sleeping.
      Chorus

3   Every child is a gift of the Lord,
    Those we love a great joy and a blessing,
    It is great to be blessed of the Lord,
    It's the life with which no one can quarrel.
      Chorus

170

1 Faithful vigil ended,
Watching, waiting cease;
Master, grant Thy servant
His discharge in peace.

2 All Thy Spirit promised,
All the Father willed,
Now these eyes behold it
Perfectly fulfilled.

3 This Thy great deliverance
Sets Thy people free;
Christ their light uplifted
All the nations see.

4 Christ, Thy people's glory!
Watching, doubting cease;
Grant to us Thy servants
Our discharge in peace.
© T. Dudley-Smith 1967   *By kind permission*

171

1 Glory give to God in heaven;
In the highest, glory be!
And on earth there's truest peace for
Men with whom the Father's pleased.
    So we praise You, worship, bless You,
    Thank You for Your love so great.
    Heavenly King, Almighty Father,
    Lord and God we praise Your name!

2 Lamb of God in triumph seated,
Jesus Christ our great high priest,
By Your all-sufficient offering
You have cancelled all our sins.
    So through You we come with boldness,
    Fearless, to the Father's throne.
    Justified by faith, rejoicing,
    Lord and God we praise Your name!

3 Holy Spirit, Lord, proceeding
From the Father and the Son,
You're the seal of our salvation.
Live and reign within our hearts.

Father, Son and Holy Spirit,
You alone are God Most High.
Maker, Saviour, Sanctifier,
Lord and God we praise Your name!

Alternative to Verse 2

Lamb of God, Messiah, Jesus
God the Father's only Son,
Pity us, have mercy on us
You who takes away our sins.
    You remove the world's offences,
    Hear us Lord. Receive our prayer.
    Pity us, have mercy on us,
    You who sits at God's right hand.

172

1   When I see the sunshine, when I see the rain,
    When I see the things that grow, that feeling
        comes again,
    And I know, yes I know,
        When I see these things, I know
    That there's a God of love, and He made these
        things I know.

2   When I see a little child, when it opens eyes,
    When I see that smiling face, and even when it
        cries.
    I know, yes I know,
        When I see a child I know,
    That there's a God of love, and He made us all
        I know.
    When I'm feeling lonely and blue
    O I know God is waiting, and I know He'll pull
        me through.
    I know that He can do it, because He did it once
        before
    When I first came to Jesus,
    O yes I know, I know He's mine for ever more
    And I know, I know He's mine for ever more.

173

1 God created the heaven and earth,
   God created the day and night:
   God created the land and the seas
   God created the grass and the trees—
      He is high over the world,
      God is high over the world,
      He is high over the world
      God is high over the world.

2 God created the seasons,
   God created the stars:
   God created the fish and the fowl
   God created the cattle and beasts—
      He is high over the world . . .

3 God created man and woman,
   In His image from the dust:
   And His power is yet the same
   If in Him we'll put our trust—
      He is high over the world . . .
   © R. J. Mills 1969 *By kind permission*

174

   Start with Chorus
   They say He's wonderful,
   They say He's wonderful,
   The sun, the moon, the stars that shine
   The sun, the moon, the stars that shine
   Say God is wonderful.

1 He makes the rain to fall,
   He sees the wheat grow tall,
   The root, the shoot and soon the fruit
   The root, the shoot and soon the fruit
   It shows He cares for all.
      Chorus

2 When I see babies small,
   And I hear children call,
   And think of family life and fun,
   And think of family life and fun,
   I know He's behind it all.
      Chorus

3   The love men have for Him
       Such love death cannot dim,
       Of small and great of rich and poor,
       Of small and great of rich and poor,
       Love like this comes from Him.
         Chorus

4   And I know He's wonderful,
       I know He's wonderful,
       The Son of God who died for me
       The Son of God who died for me
       I know He's wonderful.
         Chorus

175

1   Many wonder if there is a God
       And, if so, what He's saying to us,
       Yet though much we do not understand
       We can find Him and see in His light.
       Chorus
       God is there! Hallelujah!
       And in Jesus we're His!
       God is there! Hallelujah!
       And in Jesus we're His!

2   Satan offers his own happiness
       And we're tempted to turn from the Lord
       Yet we know that such happiness fades
       Without God we are helpless and poor.
         Chorus

3   Men make wars in this sin-ridden world
       Men have hearts in which selfishness reigns
       Men so often refuse to forgive
       Yet God loves us in spite of it all.
         Chorus

4   God was there when the world first began
       He'll be there when it passes away
       Everything is dependent on Him
       God is there just wherever we are.
         Chorus

176

1 I love the flowers, I love the trees,
   Most of all I love daisies,
   I love the rivers and the mountains high,
   But I don't love as much as God.
   Because God so loved the world that He gave
     His only Son,
   And if you believe, you can live for ever more.

2 Each mother loves her naughty child,
   Doesn't matter if he's wild,
   She's forgiving, loving, mild.
   But she don't love as much as God.
   Because God so loved the world that He gave
     His only Son,
   And if you believe, you can live for ever more.

3 See a couple hand in hand,
   Walking barefoot through the sand,
   A loving girl and a loving man
   But they don't love as much as God.
   Because God so loved the world that He gave
     His only Son.
   And if you believe, you can live for ever more.
   You can live for ever more.

© G. McClelland *By kind permission*

177

1 Lord, You sometimes speak in wonders
   Unmistakable and clear;
   Mighty signs to prove Your presence,
   Overcoming doubt and fear.

2 Lord, You sometimes speak in whispers,
   Still and small and scarcely heard;
   Only those who want to listen
   Catch the all-important word.

3 Lord, You sometimes speak in silence,
   Through our loud and noisy day;
   We can know and trust You better
   When we quietly wait and pray.

4　Lord, You often speak in Scripture—
　　Words that summon from the page,
　　Shown and taught us by Your Spirit
　　With fresh light for every age.

5　Lord, You always speak in Jesus,
　　Always new yet still the same;
　　Teach us now more of our Saviour;
　　Make our lives display His Name.

© C. Idle   *By kind permission*

178

1　Father who formed the family of man,
　　High throned in heaven, evermore the same,
　　Our prayer is still, as Christian prayer began,
　　That hallowed be Your Name.

2　Lord of all lords, the only King of kings,
　　Before whose countenance all speech is dumb,
　　Hear the one song the new creation sings—
　　Your promised Kingdom come.

3　Father of mercy, righteousness and love,
　　Shown in the sending of that only Son,
　　We ask on earth, as in the realms above,
　　Your perfect will be done.

4　Lord of the harvest and the living seed,
　　The Father's gift from which the world is fed,
　　To us Your children grant for every need
　　This day our daily bread.

5　Father, whose Son ascended now in heaven
　　Gave once Himself upon a cross to win
　　Man's whole salvation, as we have forgiven,
　　Forgive us all our sin.

6　Lord of all might and majesty and power,
　　Our true Deliverer and our great Reward,
　　From every evil, and the tempter's hour,
　　Deliver us, good Lord.

7   Father, who formed the family of man,
      Yours is the glory heaven and earth adore,
      The kingdom and the power, since time began,
      Now and for ever more.

179

If God desires it, all the flow'rs on earth will be red,
If God desires it all the stones will turn into bread,
If God allows it we can play
With moon and stars and milky way
Or shoot our rockets into space
And join the exploration race
Until He says 'It is enough'
'Til He says 'It is enough'.

Why can't we affect the pattern of the day
    and night?
Why can't we stop flowers fading—losing their
    delight?
Why can't we decide to put the clocks of time into
    reverse?
And relive our lives again for better or for worse?
Yet if we really could
Would it be for our good?
Much better that our ways belong to Him who
    understands—
Much better that our destiny is safely in His hands.

If God desires it, all the flowers on earth will be red,
If God desires it all the stones will turn into bread,
If God allows it we can play
With moon and stars and milky way
Or shoot our rockets into space
And join the exploration race
Until He says 'It is enough'.
'Til He says 'It is enough'.

180

The hills in their beauty His splendour have shown.
The rivers in torrent His greatness made known.
Yet from all these wonders God chose man alone
To be with Him each day.
But man in his blindness has gone astray,
Forsaken God's law, despising God's way.
But all was forgiven, that glorious day
When He died for me.

© D. Kennedy 1969   *By kind permission*

181

1 Beyond the grasp of human brain,
   Great God, majestic Ruler,
   We men by faith, your presence find
   In Christ, our risen Master.
   And all the pow'r which we can use
   Through turbine, jet and motor
   Is nothing to the power of Christ
   Who frees us from disaster.

2 For we believe, despite the power
   Of greed and lust and Satan
   Which dominates the wills of men,
   That sin can be forgiven.
   In humble trust and confidence
   No power our souls can frighten
   We spread your liberating truth
   That speaks of love in heaven.

3 Yet here, within your universe,
   We struggle with the Tempter
   He has no right to trick and trap,
   No right to make us cower.
   So, Spirit of the living Christ,
   The Saviour and the Victor,
   That we may daily overcome
   Uphold us with your power.

© M. Saward 1969   *By kind permission*

182

1 The future now is dark, the path unknown;
   God's people walk in night and seem alone.
   When will the promised time come, and it all be
       shown—
   God in control—God on the throne?

2 Though nations rise and fall and kingdoms sway,
Though wars and tumults rage day after day;
His promise stands though heaven and earth
    may pass away;
His word remains—true for today.

3 How much we need His Word in hours like
    these!
More powerful than the threats of enemies;
Above the raging of the storms and mighty
    seas—
He is the Lord, He holds the keys.

4 Of life and death and hell, and every throne,
He only holds the keys and He alone;
Of heaven and glory and of all eternities,
He is the Lord—He holds the keys.
© D. Green   *By kind permission*

183

1 God is all-loving—He has redeemed me
God is all-loving—And He loves me.
    Chorus
    And so I sing again God is all-loving
    God is all-loving—And He loves me.

2 I lay in bondage to sin's dominion
And as I lay I could not get free.
    Chorus

3 I lay within the death-grip of Satan
Sin pays its servants wages of death
    Chorus

4 But He sent Jesus, to be our Saviour
But He sent Jesus, who set me free.
    Chorus

5 By pledge of pardon He loosed my burden
His Holy Spirit lifted my load.
    Chorus

6 Your love is patient with my shortcomings
Your love upholds me in all my need.
    Chorus

7 Your joy refreshes my fainting spirit
   Your peace envelops my troubled heart.
    Chorus

8 Now I inherit eternal riches
   Through You inherit eternal rest.
    Chorus

9 O love eternal, I'll ever praise You
   For ever more Your love I'll proclaim.
    Chorus

184

1 From Bethlehem to Calvary
   From the crib to the cruel tree,
   From despair to joy for me,
   There is only Jesus.

2 Oh, Jesus, Your love is so great to me
   That it reaches the depths of my heart.
   Oh Jesus, Your love, all Your love for me,
   Makes my fear and my sorrow depart.

3 I want ev'ryone to know
   Of the One who loves me so
   Christ alone can set them free
   And Him they'll praise with me.

4 From Bethlehem to Calvary,
   From the crib to the cruel tree,
   From despair to joy for me,
   There is only Jesus.

185

1 Christ is the Lord of the smallest atom,
   Christ is the Lord of outer space,
   Christ is the Lord of the constellations,
   Christ is the Lord of ev'ry place;
     Of the furthest star,
     Of the coffee bar,
     Of the length of the Berlin Wall;
     Of the village green,
     Of the Asian scene,
     Christ is the Lord of all;

Christ is the Lord of the human heartbeat,
Christ is the Lord of ev'ry breath,
Christ is the Lord of a man's existence,
Christ is the Lord of life and death.

2   Christ is the Lord of our thoughts and feelings,
Christ is the Lord of all we plan,
Christ is the Lord of a man's decision,
Christ is the Lord of total man;
    In the local street,
    Where the people meet,
    In the church or the nearby hall;
    In the factory,
    In the family,
    Christ is the Lord of all;
Christ is the Lord of our love and courtship,
Christ is the Lord of man and wife,
Christ is the Lord of the things we care for,
Christ is the Lord of all our life.

© K. Preston *By kind permission*

186

1   Who took fish and bread, hungry people fed?
Who changed water into wine?
Who made well the sick, who made see
    the blind?
Who touched earth with feet divine?
    Only Jesus, Only Jesus, Only He has done
        this:
    Who made live the dead? Truth and kindness
        spread?
    Only Jesus did all this.

2   Who walked dusty road? Cared for young and
    old?
Who sat children on His knee?
Who spoke words so wise? Filled men with
    surprise,
Who gave all, but charged no fee?
    Only Jesus, Only Jesus, Only He has done
        this:
    Who in death and grief spoke peace to a
        thief?
    Only Jesus did all this.

3 Who soared through the air? Joined His Father
     there?
   He has you and me in view:
   He, who this has done, is God's only Son,
   And He's int'rested in you.
       Only Jesus, Only Jesus, Only He has done
         this:
       He can change a heart, give a new fresh start,
       Only He can do this.

© R. J. Mills 1969 *By kind permission*

187

1 I've tried in vain a thousand ways
   My fears to quiet, my hopes to raise:
   But what I need, the Bible says,
   Is ever only Jesus.

2 He died, He lives, He reigns, He pleads,
   There's love in all His work and deeds;
   There's all a guilty sinner needs
   For evermore in Jesus.

3 For all things work together for good
   With those who love and serve the Lord:
   I'll trust in Him for all I need.
   For evermore in Jesus.

4 In times like these, it can be hard
   To lift the cross and follow my Lord
   But He is with us, day by day,
   This never-failing Jesus.

© (Verses 1-2) Charles M. Alexander Copyrights Trust;
(Verses 3-4) R. J. Mayor 1969 *By kind permission*

188

1 Through all our days we'll sing the praise
   Of Christ, the resurrected,
   Who, though divine, did not decline
   To be by men afflicted.
   Pain, pain, and suffering,
   He knew its taste, He bore its sting;
   Peace, peace to men on earth,
   Through Christ our King and Saviour!

2   His birth obscure, His family poor,
    He owned no crown, no kingdom.
    Yet men who grope in darkness, hope
    Since He brought light and freedom.
    Shame, shame, and agony
    Though guiltless He of felony;
    Shout, shout, His sinless name,
    Our Jesus, King and Saviour!

3   At fearful cost His life He lost
    That death might be defeated.
    The Man of Love, now risen above
    In majesty is seated.
    Low, low, was His descent
    To men by sin and sorrow bent;
    Life, life to all who trust
    The Lord, our King and Saviour!

4   And all who trust will find they must
    Obey the will of heaven,
    For grief intense can make some sense
    To men who've been forgiven.
    Hard, hard the road He trod
    The Son of Man, the Son of God;
    Hope, hope, in Christ alone,
    Our reigning King and Saviour!

© M. Saward 1967 *By kind permission*

189

Start with Chorus
O, let us sing of our merciful King,
Mighty Redeemer is He;
We give Him praise for His wonderful ways,
Goodness so loving and free.

1   He leads His wandering children along,
    Giving their troubled hearts rest;
    He giveth peace to the hungry soul,
    Lifting him out of distress.
        Chorus

2   If you are weary and crushed with despair,
    When Satan's power is strong,
    Call to the One whom the foe must shun,
    He'll give you strength and a song!
        Chorus

3   He breaks the fetters of sorrow and sin,
    Raising men out of their plight,
    He calms the waves on the stormy sea,
    He turns the darkness to light.
        Chorus

4   He turns the wilderness into a well,
    The barren land into a plain,
    He makes the trusting and humble rejoice,
    Giving them gladness again.
        Chorus
© L. C. Taylor   *By kind permission*

190

1   Wonderful Jesus our Lord, wonderful King,
    To You our praises outpoured, loudly we sing;
    Trumpet notes richly scored,
    Strong beat and crashing chord,
    For Jesus Christ our Lord, our God and King.

2   Christ Jesus, Saviour and God, ruling on high,
    Lonely the pathway You trod, destined to die,
    Bearing our load of pain,
    Now gone above to reign,
    Glorious Son of God, Victor on high.

3   We praise You Jesus our Lord, Saviour and
        Friend,
    For You our thanks we record. Joy without end.
    Salvation's free reward,
    Pardon and peace restored,
    All from the Cross outpoured, wonderful Friend.
© J. B. Foote   *By kind permission*

191

1   Christ the Light who shines unfading
    In the sad, sin-darkened mind;
    Guiding those who grope in error,
    Opening eyes that sin made blind;
        Shows Himself the Lord of Glory
        Shining for a lost mankind.

2   Christ the Bread who came from heaven
    Hungry souls to satisfy:
    Just as loaves must first be broken,
    Our Life-giver had to die;
        Made Himself a generous Offering,
        Gave Himself for our supply.

3   Christ the Life who rose in splendour
    From the cold and dismal cave,
    On the Resurrection morning
    Conquered death and burst His grave;
        Showed Himself the mighty Champion,
        Still alive and strong to save.

4   Christ the King, to earth returning,
    Surely will not long delay;
    Christ the Son of God requires us
    Now to trust Him and obey;
        Stands Himself as Lord and Saviour,
        Asking our response today.

© C. Idle 1969 *By kind permission*

192

1   Hush little Baby, don't You cry,
    Remember, Jesus, You were born to die.
        All Your trials, Lord, soon be over.

2   To Your world You came, a Jew;
    But even they rejected You.
        All Your trials, Lord, soon be over.

3   On Your cross You gave this cry,
    'My God, I am forsaken, why?'
        All Your trials, Lord, soon be over.

4   You died, my Master, You died,
    Bu You rose again.
        All Your trials, Lord, soon be over.

5   How can I so careless be,
    Of love which suffered so for me?
        All Your trials, Lord, soon be over.

6   Teach me Lord to love men too;
    If they laugh at me, they did worse to You.
        All our trials, Lord, soon be over.

7   Word hard, my brothers, work fast,
    For He's coming soon.
        Then our trials, Lord, shall be over!
© P. Malloch 1969 *By kind permission*

193

1   He is the Way—the end of all my searching;
    He is the Truth—I'll trust His every word;
    He is the Life abundant, everlasting;
    This is the Christ, the Saviour of the world.

2   More of the Way—dear Lord, be this my
        choosing;
    More of the Truth—Lord, teach me day by
        day;
    More of the Life—for ever satisfying;
    More of Thyself—the Life, the Truth, the Way!
© G. Brattle 1969 *By kind permission*

194

1   I know a name
    That's never gonna pass away,
    Though men may try 'n' try 'n' try to forget it,
    God will never let it die.
        Jesus—that's the name.
        Son of God who came to die for me.
        Jesus—that's the name.

2   God said this name
    Would always be remembered here,
    Here in this world that turned Him away,
    Men would always pray to Him.
        Jesus—that's the name,
        He who took the blame for all my sins,
        Jesus—that's the name.

3   And do you know Him, this Jesus, as your
        own living Lord?
    If you want to know this Jesus believe His
        faithful word.
    If you call Him then be certain that your voice
        will be heard,
    He'll come to you, make you free.

4 Then you will know
   The name that's never gonna die.
   Then you'll be one of those who pray day
      by day,
   One of those who say like me—
      Jesus—that's the name,
      Let me spread His fame until He comes,
   Jesus—that's the name.

195

1 There was a man from Galilee
   He came to die for you and me.
   He gave his life on Calvary
   And now He lives for you and me.
   I know He lives in me.

2 God sent His Son, His only one,
   To show us love from up above
   To show the way and how to pray
   And how He cares for us each day.
   I know He cares for me.

3 In such a world so full of sin
   Where can we find real peace within
   Where can we find our rock secure
   Where can we find a love so pure?
   Christ is the only one.

196

1 Jesus from glory to Bethlehem came,
   Born in a small wayside inn;
   He who created the worlds by His pow'r
   In grace came to save us from sin.

2 Jesus the Word to His own people came,
   Their true Redeemer and King,
   Him they rejected, His truth they despised,
   They spurned all the gifts He would bring.

3 Jesus the Saviour to Calvary came,
   Victim of hatred and strife;
   Flogged and disowned He was nailed to a cross,
   And yet by that death we have life.

4 Jesus the Lord out of death's bondage came,
  Victor o'er Satan and sin,
  Now in His pow'r He will dwell in our lives,
  And helps us our victory to win.

5 Jesus the Master to your life will come,
  Bringing salvation and peace;
  In His glad service you'll find your reward
  And pleasures that never shall cease.

6 Jesus the Sovereign in glory shall come,
  Man's full redemption to bring;
  Saints of all ages their Lord shall acclaim,
  Their Saviour, their God and their King.

© J. E. Seddon 1969 *By kind permission*

197

1 There is no-one in the world like Jesus,
  There is none that can compare with my Lord
  Loving us, saving us,
  Knowing us, keeping us,
  Faithful Shepherd, gracious Friend.
  There is no-one in the world like Jesus,
  There is none that can compare with my Lord.

2 If I go up to the heavens He is there
  If I go down to the depths He's there too
  Anywhere, everywhere,
  Anytime, all the time,
  He is with me evermore.
  There is no-one in the world like Jesus,
  There is none that can compare with my Lord.

3 Nothing in this world can ever separate
  The believer from the love of the Lord.
  Death or life, evil powers,
  Present things, coming things,
  None can part us from His love.
  There is no-one in the world like Jesus,
  There is none that can compare with my Lord.

© M. A. Baughen 1969 *By kind permission*

198

1 King of kings and Prince of princes,
   Greatest joy that came to earth,
   Wondrous love our lives encircling,
   Christ divine of Holy Birth.
   On His knee He took the children
   At His feet the oxen bowed,
   From His face there shone a radiance,
   Brighter than the whitest cloud.

2 With His precious Blood He saved us,
   On His head He wore a thorn,
   By His hands He hung and suffered,
   Round Him was a cloak all torn.
   With the Father now, in heaven,
   Jesus is enthroned on high,
   'Hallelujah', sing the angels,
   'See the King of kings is nigh!'

© D. Brand 1969 *By kind permission*

199

1 Within a crib my Saviour lay,
   A wooden manger filled with hay,
   Come down for love on Christmas Day,
      All glory be to Jesus!

2 Upon a cross my Saviour died,
   To ransom sinners crucified,
   His loving arms still open wide,
      All glory be to Jesus!

3 A victor's crown my Saviour won,
   His work of love and mercy done,
   The Father's high-ascended Son,
      All glory be to Jesus!

© T. Dudley-Smith *By kind permission*

200

1 Holy Child, how still You lie;
   Safe the manger, soft the hay,
   Faint upon the Eastern sky
   Breaks the dawn of Christmas Day.

2 Holy Child, whose birth day brings
   Shepherds from their field and fold,
   Angel choirs and Eastern kings,
   Myrrh and frankincense and gold.

3 Holy Child, what gift of grace,
   From the Father freely willed
   In Your infant form we trace
   All God's promises fulfilled.

4 Holy Child, whose human years
   Span like ours delight and pain,
   One in human joys and tears,
   One in all but sin and stain.

5 Holy Child, so far from home,
   Sons of men to seek and save,
   To what dreadful death You come,
   To what dark and silent grave.

6 Holy Child, before whose Name
   Powers of darkness faint and fall;
   Conquered, death and sin and shame,
   Jesus Christ is Lord of all.

7 Holy Child, how still You lie;
   Safe the manger, soft the hay,
   Clear upon the Eastern sky
   Breaks the dawn of Christmas Day.

© T. Dudley-Smith 1966 *By kind permission*

201

1 See Him a-lying on a bed of straw;
   A draughty stable with an open door,
   Mary cradling the babe she bore;
   The Prince of Glory is His name.

        Chorus
        O now carry me to Bethlehem
        To see the Lord appear to men:
        Just as poor as was the stable then,
        The Prince of Glory when He came.

2 Star of silver sweep across the skies,
   Show where Jesus in the manger lies.
   Shepherds swiftly from your stupor rise
   To see the Saviour of the world.
        Chorus

3   Angels, sing again the song you sang,
     Bring God's glory to the heart of man.
     Sing that Bethl'em's little baby can
     Be Salvation to the soul.
          Chorus

4   Mine are riches—from Thy poverty;
     From Thine innocence, eternity;
     Mine, forgiveness by Thy death for me,
     Child of sorrow for my joy.
          Chorus

© M. A. Perry *by kind permission*

202

1   A baby was born in Bethlehem
     By a stable light:
     A stranger in occupied country
     On a winter night—
          But the road runs from Bethlehem
          Straight and stony,
          Steep and long:
          The road runs from Bethlehem
          Through thirty years
          To Calvary.

2   The baby born in Bethlehem
     Was Jesus Christ, God's Son,
     And when as man our Saviour came
     Redemption was begun—
          But the road runs . . .

3   For He was born in Bethlehem
     Under a winter sky
     To walk the road to Calvary
     There for our sins to die—
          And the road runs . . .

© P. Monk 1969 *By kind permission*

203

1   O come, O come, Immanuel,
     And ransom captive Israel,
     That mourns in lonely exile here,
     Until the Son of God appear.

Refrain
Rejoice, Rejoice! Immanuel
Shall come to thee, O Israel.

2 O come, O come, Thou Lord of might
Who to Thy tribes, on Sinai's height,
In ancient times didst give the law
In cloud and majesty and awe:
Refrain

3 O come, Thou Rod of Jesse, free
Thine own from Satan's tyranny;
From depths of hell Thy people save,
And give them victory o'er the grave:
Refrain

4 O come, Thou Dayspring, come and cheer
Our spirits by Thine advent here;
Disperse the gloomy clouds of night,
And death's dark shadows put to flight:
Refrain

5 O come, Thou Key of David, come
And open wide our heavenly home;
Make safe the way that leads on high,
And close the path to misery:
Refrain

204

1 In between
The hotel and the road.
In a borrowed stable,
The King comes as foretold.
The man in the middle
Is the one who came for us,
As a baby in a cradle—
And we nailed Him to a cross.

2 In between
A donkey and a cow,
In a borrowed manger,
The King descends so low.
The man in the middle, &c.

3   In between
    The husband and the wife,
    In a borrowed fam'ly,
    The King takes on our life.
            The man in the middle, &c.

4   In between
    The shepherds and the kings;
    Without the borrowed riches
    The King new value brings.
            The man in the middle, &c.

5   In between
    Two crosses on a hill,
    On a borrowed gallows
    For us He pays the bill.
            The man in the middle, &c.

© R. A. Leaver   *By kind permission*

205

1   Hush you, my baby,
    The night wind is cold.
    The lambs from the hillside
    Are safe in the fold.
    Sleep with the starlight
    And wake with the morn,
        The Lord of all glory
    A baby is born.

2   Hush you, my baby,
    So soon to be grown,
    Watching by moonlight
    On mountain alone,
    Toiling and travelling—
    So sleep while you can,
        Till the Lord of all glory
    Is seen as a man.

3   Hush you, my baby,
    The years will not stay;
    The cross on the hilltop
    The end of the way.
    Dim through the darkness,
    In grief and in gloom,
        The Lord of all glory
    Lies cold in the tomb.

4 Hush you, my baby,
The Father on high
In power and dominion
The darkness puts by.
Bright from the shadows,
The seal and the stone,
  The Lord of all glory
Returns to His own.

5 Hush you, my baby,
The sky turns to gold;
The lambs on the hillside
Are loose from the fold.
Fast fades the midnight
And new springs the morn,
  For the Lord of all glory
A Saviour is born.

© T. Dudley-Smith 1968 *By kind permission*

206

In a little town, at early dawn,
Before the grip of night had well-nigh gone,
In a stable bare in Mary's care and Joseph's,
There my Lord was born.
On a night like this, with its starry sky,
Some shepherds had no time to wonder why
A brilliant light out of the night, dazzled their
  sight,
And angels cry:
'Don't be afraid, but rather joy;
To you this tide is born a boy.'
And now the message is unfurled,
'He came as Saviour to the world.'
And yet this baby had to die,
To save a guilty sinner such as I;
And this because upon the cross
He'd take my sins at Calvary.

© S. Beckley *By kind permission*

207

1 Christmas for God's holy people
Is a time of joy and peace,
So, good Christian men and women
Hymns and carols let us raise
To our God
Come to earth
Son of man, by human birth.

2   Child of Mary, virgin mother,
      Peasant baby, yet our king,
      Cradled once midst ass and oxen
      Joyful carols now we sing
      To our God
      Come to earth
      Son of man, by human birth.

3   Angel armies sang in chorus
      To our Christ's nativity
      He who came to share our nature
      So we sing with gaiety
      To our God
      Come to earth
      Son of man, by human birth.

4   Working men ran to the manger,
      Saw the babe of Bethlehem,
      Glorified the God in heaven,
      Now we join to sing with them
      To our God
      Come to earth
      Son of man, by human birth.

5   Infant lowly born in squalor,
      Prophet, King and great High Priest
      Word of God to man descending
      Still we sing, both great and least
      To our God
      Come to earth
      Son of man, by human birth.

© M. Saward 1966 *By kind permission*

208

1   When I survey the wondrous cross
      On which the Prince of Glory died,
      My richest gain I count but loss,
      And pour contempt on all my pride.

2   Forbid it, Lord, that I should boast
      Save in the cross of Christ my God;
      All the vain things that charm me most,
      I sacrifice them to His blood.

3 See, from His head, His hands, His feet,
   Sorrow and love flow mingled down;
   Did e'er such love and sorrow meet,
   Or thorns compose so rich a crown?

4 Were the whole realm of nature mine,
   That were an offering far too small;
   Love so amazing, so divine,
   Demands my soul, my life, my all.

209

1 Long years ago in a far Eastern land,
   a man died,
   Nails in His hands and His feet and a
   sword in His side,
   Crowds watched Him die, as He hung on
   a cross in the gloom.
   When they took Him down, His body was
   sealed in a tomb.

   Chorus
   A man died, a man died,
   Nails in His hands and His feet and a
   sword in His side.

2 The man had said 'after three days I rise
   from the dead'—
   His enemies the Jews now remembered
   what He had said.
   They wanted a guard for the tomb for they
   still feared the man,
   'Go your way', said Pilate, 'and make it as safe
   as you can.'
   Chorus

3 So soldiers set watch on the tomb all day and
   all night,
   And on the third day, the women came ere it
   was light,
   They found the tomb open, no soldiers,
   the body was gone,
   And inside were two angels who said
   'He is risen—God's Son'.
   Chorus

4   The Jews did not find Him, and death could
      not hold Him, nor the grave,
    For this man is Jesus, Messiah, Almighty to
      save
    He was mocked by the crowd, as He died on
      the cross for their sin,
    But He rose from the dead, a sure hope for
      all now to win.
        Chorus

5   What is He to you, this Jesus who died in
      such shame?
    Your Saviour? A good man? Or merely a
      story-book name?
    Own Him as your Saviour, your lips with
      His praises will ring,
    For one day you must meet Him, as either
      your Judge or your King.
        Chorus

210

1   On the tree on the hill called Skull,
    Christ Jesus died alone,
    Just He was, and good, and God,
    That's why He was alone.

2   Not that we cared or tried to stop,
    Those who spat in the face
    Of the man
    On the tree on the Hill called Skull,
    Who died there in our place.

3   On the tree on the Hill called Skull
    Christ Jesus won the fight,
    The battle then was with Hell,
    So day turned black as night.

4   Not that we knew or asked Him to
    In fact we put Him there
    Yes, the man
    On the tree on the Hill called Skull,
    Who stripped the Devil bare.

5 On the tree on the Hill called Skull,
   Christ Jesus ripped apart,
   That veil which cuts us off from God,
   Our selfish wilful heart.

6 Not that we touched or even reached
   For the friendship of our God
   In the man
   On the tree on the Hill called Skull,
   Whose nail-pierced hand says 'Come'.

7 On the tree on the Hill called Skull,
   Christ Jesus once for all,
   Put the world to rights that hour,
   'It's finished' was His last call.

8 Not that we wanted it quite that free
   With nothing more to pay
   To the man
   On the tree on the Hill called Skull
   Whose death gives life today.

© R. Warren   *By kind permission*

211

1 A hill beside Jerusalem,
   Three crosses stark and free,
   Mark the place where three men slowly died—
   And one there died for you and me.

2 They hailed Him at Jerusalem's gate,
   And gathered there to see
   The Son of God come riding in—
   But there He died for you and me.

3 A friend betrayed Him to the Jews,
   But death He would not flee;
   They scorned and mocked and spat on Him,
   And there He died for you and me.

4 They led Him up to Calvary's hill,
   And nailed Him to a tree,
   They pierced His side with cruel spear—
   And there He died for you and me.

5 But death our Saviour could not hold,
For God's own Son was He,
He rose victorious over sin,
Because He died for you and me.

© C. E. Reddin *By kind permission*

212

Jesus came down to earth from heav'n above;
Yes He came down to earth. Wonderful love!
Do you remember long ago?
Do you remember, He loved us so.

1 He didn't have to come for you and me,
He wanted us to live eternally,
Do you remember, though you weren't there?
Do you remember, or don't you care,
    don't you care?
  Is it nothing to you that Jesus died?
  Is it nothing that He was crucified?
  Can't you believe? Can't you believe?

2 He didn't have to die on Calvary;
He wanted us to live eternally.
Do you remember, long ago?
Do you remember? He loved us so, loved us so!
  Is it nothing to you that Jesus died?
  Is it nothing that He was crucified?
  Can't you believe? Can't you believe?

Do you remember though you weren't there?
Do you remember, or don't you care?
Don't you care, don't you care, don't you care,
    don't you care?
Do you remember?

© Sky Sounds *By kind permission*

213

1 A purple robe, a crown of thorn,
A reed in His right hand;
Before the soldiers' spite and scorn
I see my Saviour stand.

2 He bears between the Roman guard
The weight of all our woe;
A stumbling figure bowed and scarred
I see my Saviour go.

3 Fast to the cross's spreading span,
High in the sunlit air,
All the unnumbered sins of man
I see my Saviour bear.

4 He hangs, by whom the world was made,
Beneath the darkened sky;
The everlasting ransom paid,
I see my Saviour die.

5 He shares on high His Father's throne,
Who once in mercy came;
For all His love to sinners shown
I sing my Saviour's Name.

© T. Dudley-Smith 1968 *By kind permission*

214

1 O Sacrifice of Calvary,
O Lamb whose sacred blood was shed,
O great High Priest on heaven's throne,
O Victor from the dead.
Here I recall Your agony
Here see again Your bloodstained brow
Beyond the sign of Bread and Wine
I know Your presence now.

2 No longer, Saviour, do You plead
Your glorious sacrifice unique,
Yet, Lord, in heaven intercede
While I Your mercy seek.
Before Your Holy Table laid
I kneel once more in love and peace,
Your Blood and Flesh my soul refresh
With joy that shall not cease.

© M. Saward 1968 *By kind permission*

215

1 'This do' the Master said,
'This sacrament repeat,
My Body and my Blood
In holy symbol eat.
To this great feast
I will invite,
And here unite,
Both great and least.'

2   Don't come, if you would boast
    Your knowledge and your might,
    Don't come, if you refuse
    To serve the Lord of Light.
    But those whose sin
    Has been confessed
    May take their rest
    And join herein.

3   For you, whose sin He bore
    A promise He provides,
    His covenant He makes
    And at His board presides.
    His Sacrifice
    He'll not repeat,
    But take and eat,
    And count the price.

4   One loaf, one body, we,
    One family divine,
    In sweet communion feed
    Upon that Bread and Wine.
    The Great High Priest,
    Until He come
    Has now become
    Our heavenly feast.

5   Then lift Your Church to heaven
    Where hunger is no more,
    And through eternity,
    O Christ, we shall adore.
    So make us share
    In glad embrace
    Your matchless grace,
    Both here and there.

© M. Saward 1962 *By kind permission*

216

1   Bright dawned the morning on Gethsemane's
    cave,
    Mary Magdalene came to weep at the grave.
    What did she find when she came full of care?
    The stone rolled away, and her Master not
    there!

Refrain
Mary, Mary weeping at the tomb,
Jesus came and took away her gloom.

2 'Where have they taken him?' poor Mary did
    pray,
   Crying, and bowing her head in dismay;
   Suddenly in front of her a shadow did fall,
   Mary raised her eyes—'tis the gardener, that's
    all.'
   Refrain

3 'Why are you weeping? Come, tell me your
    fears.'
   'My Jesus is gone', she said through her tears.
   'Mary!' was all that the Person replied,
   Then Mary knew at once that her Lord had
    not died.
   Refrain

4 Overcome with joy, she touched the hem of
   His gown,
   Clinging to Jesus, at His feet she fell down.
   'Lord, you're alive!' was all that Mary could
    say,
   'This is indeed your Resurrection Day!'
   Refrain

© D. Brand *By kind permission*

217

1 It happened in Jerusalem
  In the early spring,
  They say, God lived and died a man—
  Or some such crazy thing:
   Chorus
    For it happened very long ago
    And very far away,
    It happened much too long ago
    To make a scrap of sense today.

2 The charge they brought was blasphemy.
  The prisoner was framed,
  And Pilate washed his hands of Him—
  But why should he be blamed:
   Chorus

3 They flogged Him then and mocked Him,
   And dragged Him to the Hill
   Through jostling crowds that jeered—
   But why be troubled still:
       Chorus

4 And on that city rubbish-tip
   They nailed Him to a cross
   And left Him in the sun to die—
   But what's all that to us:
       Chorus

5 Friends left Him through the Sabbath day
   In a borrowed grave,
   On Sunday morning He had gone—
   But still what does that prove:
       Chorus

6 Alive they say He joined these friends
   And all the nail-marks saw;
   He parted from them heavenwards—
   But how can we be sure:
       Chorus

7 It happened in Jerusalem
   In the early spring,
   They say, God lived and died a man—
   Or some such crazy thing:
       Chorus
       For it happened very long ago
       And very far away . . .
       But though it happened long ago
       Couldn't it make a lot of sense today?
   © P. Monk 1969 *By kind permission*

218

       Start with Chorus
       We shall rise, we shall rise,
       On that resurrection morning we shall rise,
       We shall rise, we shall rise,
       On that resurrection morning we shall rise.

1 We shall then be with the Lord,
   We shall then be with the Lord,
   We shall then be with Him ever more.
       Chorus

2 Death has lost its sting for us
Death has lost its sting for us
Death has lost its sting for evermore.
   Chorus

3 Hallelujahs then will ring
Hallelujahs then will ring
Hallelujahs to the Lamb who died.
   Chorus

219

1 Spirit of God within me,
Possess my human frame;
Fan the dull embers of my heart,
Stir up the living flame.
Strive till that image Adam lost,
New minted and restored,
In shining splendour brightly bears
The likeness of the Lord.

2 Spirit of truth within me,
Possess my thought and mind;
Lighten anew the inward eye
By Satan rendered blind;
Shine on the words that wisdom speaks
And grant me power to see
The truth made known to men in Christ,
And in that truth be free.

3 Spirit of love within me,
Possess my hands and heart;
Break through the bonds of self-concern
That seeks to stand apart:
Grant me the love that suffers long,
That hopes, believes and bears,
The love fulfilled in sacrifice,
That cares as Jesus cares.

4 Spirit of life within me,
Possess this life of mine;
Come as the wind of heaven's breath,
Come as the fire divine!
Spirit of Christ, the living Lord,
Reign in this house of clay,
Till from its dust with Christ I rise
To everlasting day.

220

1 Fire of God, titanic Spirit,
 Burn within our hearts today,
 Cleanse our sin; may we exhibit
 Holiness in every way.
 Purge the squalidness that shames us,
 Soils the body; taints the soul.
 And through Jesus Christ who claims us,
 Purify us; make us whole.

2 Wind of God, dynamic Spirit,
 Breathe upon our hearts today
 That we may Your power inherit
 Hear us, Spirit, as we pray.
 Fill the vacuum that enslaves us,
 Emptiness of heart and soul,
 And, through Jesus Christ who saves us,
 Give us life and make us whole.

3 Voice of God, prophetic Spirit,
 Speak to every heart today,
 To encourage or prohibit,
 Urging action or delay.
 Clear the vagueness which impedes us,
 Come, enlighten mind and soul.
 And, through Jesus Christ who leads us.
 Teach the Truth that makes us whole.

© M. Saward 1968 *By kind permission*

221

1 He was there when earth was hurled in space,
 By man or beast untrod.
 He was moving over the water's face,
 The unseen Spirit of God.

   Chorus
   He's the Comforter,
   He's the breath of God,
   He's the wind of rushing mighty pow'r,
   He gives strength to win
   When He dwells within
   Making Jesus real every hour.

2 He was there of old and gave God's Word,
Inspired both sage and youth;
The apostles wrote what they'd seen and heard,
Led by the Spirit of Truth.
Chorus

3 He was there in fire on the Church outpoured,
His gifts and power sufficed;
He reminded men of their reigning Lord,
The living Spirit of Christ.
Chorus

4 He is here to give new birth, and still
The clamour and the strife;
Let us grieve Him not but seek His will,
Dynamic Spirit of Life!
Chorus

222 1 If you've asked my Jesus
To be your Saviour,
You will know the Spirit's pow'r within.
He will want to change you
To make you like your Lord
Giving you vict'ry over sin.
Chorus
Yes, guidance comes from God the
Holy Spirit
Let Him control your life from day to day;
Just seek His will in prayer
You'll find He's always there
To help you find God's perfect way.

2 Do you know the answer
To all the problems
You may have to face this very day?
Jesus sent His Spirit
To live within your heart
To hear and guide you when you pray.
Chorus

3 Is your life as useful
As God desires it?
Is He satisfied with all you do?
Seek the Spirit's guidance
And He will show you all
The Lord your God has planned for you.
Chorus

223

1 When the Lord in glory comes
   Not the trumpets, not the drums,
   Not the anthem, not the psalm,
   Not the thunder, not the calm,
   Not the shout the heavens raise,
   Not the chorus, not the praise,
   Not the silences sublime,
   Not the sounds of space and time,
   But His voice when He appears
   Shall be music to my ears.
      But His voice when He appears
      Shall be music to my ears.

2 When the Lord is seen again
   Not the glories of His reign,
   Not the lightnings through the storm,
   Not the radiance of His form,
   Not His pomp and power alone,
   Not the splendours of His throne.
   Not His robe and diadems,
   Not the gold and not the gems,
   But His face upon my sight
   Shall be darkness into light.
      But His face upon my sight
      Shall be darkness into light.

3 When the Lord to human eyes
   Shall bestride our narrow skies,
   Not the child of humble birth,
   Not the carpenter of earth,
   Not the man by men denied,
   Not the victim crucified,
   But the God who died to save,
   But the victor of the grave,
   He it is to whom I fall,
   Jesus Christ, my All in all.
      He it is to whom I fall,
      Jesus Christ, my All in all.

© T. Dudley-Smith 1967 *By kind permission*

224

He's coming; my Jesus is coming,
My Jesus is coming, He's coming for you
and me.

1 When He went away He told us to watch
   and pray,
   For He said He'd come back some day.
   He's coming for you and me.
   Chorus
   He's coming again.
   Can't you see that He died for you, and
   He died for me?
   He wants us to live eternally.
   So if heaven's not your home,
   You can take Him as your own.
   He's coming; yes Jesus is coming;
   My Jesus is coming. He's coming for you
   and me.

2 In that sudden hour we shall see Him in all
   His power.
   We won't know the day or the hour
   That's He's coming for you and me.
   But when He comes again
   Will He take you then,
   Or will He leave you here with other men?
   Now are you ready?
   Are you ready to go with Him?
   Chorus
   He's coming for you and me.

© Sky Sounds *By kind permission*

225

1 Do you ever search your heart as you watch
   the day depart?
   Is there something 'way down deep you try to
   hide?
   If this day should be the end and eternity begin,
   When the book is opened wide,
   Would the Lord be satisfied?

Chorus
Is He satisfied, is He satisfied?
Is He satisfied with me?
Have I done my best, have I stood the test?
Is He satisfied with me?
When my Lord shall come again,
When He walks and talks with men,
What if ev'ry friend He had were just
* like me?*
Would He feel a welcome here or would He
* go away in tears?*
Am I all that I should be?
Is He satisfied with me?

2 Feeble is the lamp of fame by which man
     inscribes his name
   On the walls of time for other men to see.
   Though he boasts of wealth and power, none
     can help him in that hour
   When the angels hear his plea;
   Is He satisfied with me?
     Chorus

226

1 When He comes
   When He comes
   We shall see the Lord in glory when He comes.
   As I read the gospel story
   We shall see the Lord in glory,
   We shall see the Lord in glory when He comes!
     With the Alleluias ringing to the sky,
     With the Alleluias ringing to the sky,
     As I read the gospel story
     We shall see the Lord in glory
     With the Alleluias ringing to the sky!

2 When He comes,
   When He comes,
   We shall hear the trumpet sounded when He
     comes,
   We shall hear the trumpet sounded,
   See the Lord by saints surrounded.
   We shall hear the trumpet sounded when He
     comes!

With the Alleluias ringing to the sky,
With the Alleluias ringing to the sky,
We shall hear the trumpet sounded,
See the Lord by saints surrounded,
With the Alleluias ringing to the sky!

3   When He comes,
    When He comes,
    We shall all rise up to meet Him when He
        comes.
    When He calls His own to greet Him
    We shall all rise up to meet Him,
    We shall all rise up to meet Him when He
        comes!
        With the Alleluias ringing to the sky,
        With the Alleluias ringing to the sky,
        When He calls His own to greet Him
        We shall all rise up to meet Him
        With the Alleluias ringing to the sky!

4   When He comes
    When He comes
    We shall see the Lord in glory when He comes.
    As I read the gospel story
    We shall see the Lord in glory,
    We shall see the Lord in glory when He comes!
        With the Alleluias ringing to the sky,
        With the Alleluias ringing to the sky,
        As I read the gospel story
        We shall see the Lord in glory
        With the Alleluias ringing to the sky!

© T. Dudley-Smith 1967 *By kind permission*

227

1   Once He came unrecognized,
    A man by men He was despised
    Once for our sin He was chastized:
        But . . . but . . . He shall return in glory
        But . . . but . . . He shall return as King—
            And the tongues of men and angels
            And the songs of suns and planets,
            And every voice in Creation
            Shall be His welcome then.

2   Once He had a human birth
    And lived like us upon this earth
    Knew human grief and human mirth:
        But . . . but . . . He shall return in glory
        But . . . but . . . He shall return as King—
            And sorrow banished for ever,
            And joy multiplied for ever,
            And human laughter in heaven,
            Shall be His fanfare then.

3   Once He suffered human pain,
    Felt sun and wind, the storm and rain,
    Tempted like us again and again
        But . . . but . . . He shall return in glory
        But . . . but . . . He shall return as King—
            And the earth become His footstool,
            And the sun a gem in His crown,
            And Satan thrown down defeated,
            Shall be His trophies then.

4   One He passed through agony
    Knew conflict in Gethsemane
    Then hung exposed, nailed to a tree:
        But . . . but . . . He shall return in glory
        But . . . but . . . He shall return as King—
            And all knees shall bow in His name
            Every tongue confess Him as Lord,
            And all His children around Him
            Shall be His victory then.

© P. Monk 1969 *By kind permission*

228

1   When I look around me
    This is the truth I see
    People are suffering the whole world
        through.
    I look the other way,
    Think of myself alone,
    Knowing what I ought to do.

2   When I have this world's goods—
    Standards of living high
    One of the 'haves' rather than the 'have nots',
    Grant me the grace to give,
    Open my heart in love,
    Tackling the world's trouble spots.

..e to feed the hungry
..ive the thirsty drink.
..ng for strangers and those alone.
..p me to visit all
..nose who may need a call
Helping some to make a home.

When the Son of Man comes,
All nations gathered there,
To those He welcomes He then will say:
'I assure you that your deed
To My brothers in their need
Was a deed you did to Me'.
© M. Whitten 1969 *By kind permission*

229

1 Sitting right there in your two-car home
    Watching the world go by;
Watching the refugees still roam
    Seeing the hungry die.
But there's nothing you can do
You simply say:
'I haven't got money to throw away!'
    Send the collecting man from your gate
    'But isn't the world in a dreadful state?'

2 Sitting right there in your sprung settee
Watching the TV show
Seeing the struggle to set men free
Watching it blow-by-blow.
But the cost of living is getting you down
You can't even spare a half-a-crown.
    Send the collecting man from your gate
    'But isn't the world in a dreadful state?'

3 Sitting right there in your favourite chair
After a three course meal
Seeing the suffering everywhere
Watching the wealthy steal.
But your rates go up and they freeze your pay
You can't get abroad for your holiday.
    Send the collecting man from your gate
    'But isn't the world in a dreadful state?'
© G. H. Reid 1969 *By kind permission*

230

1 Black or White, sir?
  This question relates
  To much more than coffee
  Or bread on our plates.
  It poses a choice between two extremes
  Affecting the members of our touring teams;
  Deciding who gets the pick of the jobs
  And who runs the world, the 'wogs' or
    the 'nobs'.
  It's as fiery as touchwood, we cannot ignore,
  Or think all we need is a change in the law;
  It's men's hearts that differ, some warm and
    some cold,
  Whatever the colour of skin we behold.

2 Love or hate, sir?
  I ask you to say;
  Please do not take long now,
  There's no middle way;
  Just think if you'd happened to be born
    jet-black—
  You'd want men to pay you, not give you
    the sack;
  Remember who carried the cross of our Lord:
  For he was an African forced by a sword;
  There won't be a conflict in Britain's small land,
  If different races can live hand-in-hand;
  When we get to heaven, without any doubt,
  No skin will be there to point us all out!

© G. C. H. Roberts *By kind permission*

231

1 In the Mission near the front, all is quiet:
    it is night:
  Then the guns behind the house begin to pound,
    and in their light
  The many huts of straw, the frightened faces.
    can be seen—
  The faces of the People In Between.

2   They have left their mountain dwellings,
         where they could no longer stay.
    They are sick and they are weary,
         and their children die each day,
    For there's little rice to eat, and no way of
         keeping clean—
    No comfort for the People In Between.

3   These people are not fighting men, they're
         labourers by birth.
    They only wished for peace, to share the
         good things of the earth.
    But their cattle disappeared, and the
         crops were brown, not green—
    No living for the People In Between.

4   What do they know of politics, the clash
         of East and West?
    Both promising the people that
         'Our side can serve you best'.
    But while the war drags on, it seems
         that neither side is keen
    To stop, and help the People In Between.

5   The hospital is crowded, and the orderlies are
         few.
    They carry on because they know they have a
         job to do.
    A minister was killed last week, a man of God
         who'd been
    Just trying to help the People In Between.

6   When fighting is the order, then the money's
         always there.
    But those who offer comfort find that
         Governments don't care.
    It's up to you and me to help, and show
         them that we mean
    Our pity for the People In Between—
    Have pity on the People In Between.

232

1 Tell all the world about Jesus
   Our Saviour, Lord and King;
   And let the whole creation
   Of His salvation sing.
   Tell all men of His greatness
   In nature and in grace;
   Creator and Redeemer,
   The Lord of time and space.

2 Tell all the world about Jesus
   That men in Him may find
   The joy of His forgiveness,
   True peace of heart and mind.
   Tell all men of His goodness,
   His deep, unfailing care;
   Of love so rich in mercy,
   A love beyond compare.

3 Tell all the world about Jesus
   That everyone may know
   Of His almighty triumph
   O'er every evil foe.
   Tell all men of His glory,
   When sin is overthrown,
   And He shall reign in splendour,
   The King upon His throne.

© J. E. Seddon *By kind permission*

233

Chorus
Is there an answer to it all?
Is there an answer to it all?
Can we feel at all responsible?
Listen to the wind of conscience call.

1 There's two-thirds of the world go hungry
       every night,
   Listen to the wind of conscience call,
   While we unconcerned sit and watch the
       firelight,
   Is there an answer to it all?
       Chorus

2 A man has to fight to gain his civil right,
Listen to the wind of conscience call,
While we unconcerned sit and watch the
firelight,
Is there an answer to it all?
Chorus

3 They crucified a man because they thought He
might
Make us listen to the wind of conscience call,
While we unconcerned sit and watch the
firelight,
And He is the answer to it all.

Chorus
He is the answer to it all,
He is the answer to it all,
We can all be so responsible,
He is the answer to it all;
We can all be so responsible,
Listen to the wind of conscience call.

234

1 As for our world we lift our hearts in praise,
For gifts unnumbered from our childhood days.
Now, in God's Name
Stir our compassions; give us eyes to see
The orphaned child, the starved and refugee.
The sick and lame:
For sad and needy children everywhere—
For this our world, we lift our hands in prayer.

2 As for our world we lift our hearts in praise,
The joy of home with lights and hearth ablaze,
The welcome plain;
So we recall the homeless and the cold,
The destitute, the prisoners, and the old
Who lie in pain:
For all who grieve, for all who know despair—
For this our world, we lift our hands in prayer.

3   As for our world we lift our hearts in praise,
    Recount the blessings that our life displays
        In every part,
    So look in mercy, Lord, where shadows rest,
    The ravaged homes by want and wars
        oppressed,
        The sick at heart
    With burdens more than man was meant to
        bear—
    For this our world, we lift our hands in prayer.

4   As for our world we lift our hearts in praise,
    The love of God on all our works and ways.
        So we commend
    All those who loveless live and hopeless mourn,
    Who die at last uncomforted, forlorn,
        Without a friend;
    Who own no Saviour's love, no Father's care--
    For this our world we lift our hands in prayer.

5   As for our world we lift our hearts in praise,
    So with our songs of thankfulness we raise
        This ageless plea:
    That darkened souls who have no song to sing
    May find in Christ the living Lord and King
        He came to be;
    And in His Cross and resurrection share—
    For this our world we lift our hands in prayer.

© T. Dudley-Smith 1968 *By kind permission*

235

        Meet Jesus in the morning,
        As day is breaking through;
        Meet Jesus in the noontide,
        He'll talk again with you;
        Meet Jesus in the ev'ning,
        As thoughts are turned to rest;
        Be sure to meet the Saviour,
        And ev'ry day is blest.

© G. Brattle 1969 *By kind permission*

236

Start with Chorus
It's an all-day faith you must have in
  your Lord,
It's an all-day faith you must have in
  your Lord,
It's an all-day faith you must have in
  your Lord,
For He loves you all the day long.

1 In the quiet of the morning give some time
     to Him,
   Praying that He will enrich you within,
   Forgive and deliver you from all of your sin;
   Yes, the morning you must give to your Lord.
     Chorus

2 In the heat of the noon-day put your faith in
     your God,
   Knowing that He's there as your Staff and
     your Rod,
   As you walk in the Way, tread the steps that
     He trod;
   Yes, the noon-day you must give to your Lord.
     Chorus

3 In the cool of the evening commune with
     the Son,
   Telling Him all about all you have done,
   Sharing your sorrows and recounting
     your fun;
   Yes, the evening you must give to your Lord.
     Chorus

© D Brand 1966 *By kind permission*

237

1 Hands of Jesus, take the bread,
   As long ago
   While here below;
   Take the bread at morning time.

2 Hands of Jesus, bless the bread;
   Bless it to me,
   That it may be
   Living bread at morning time.

3   Hands of Jesus, break the bread,
    And break it small,
    And grant to all
    Broken bread at morning time.

4   Hands of Jesus, give the bread,
    That with Thy Word,
    We may be fed;
    Hear our prayer at morning time.

Note: The word 'evening' may be substituted for
'morning' whenever appropriate.
© G. Brattle 1969 *By kind permission*

238

1   Open my ears to Your Word
    Lord of my life, I pray,
    That as I seek to serve You
    I may hear what You say.

2   Open my eyes to Your Word
    That as I read each day,
    New things I may discover
    To help me walk Your way.

3   Open my heart to Your Word
    That as I read today
    My heart may not be hardened
    But will with joy obey.
© S. N. Davies 1969 *By kind permission*

239

Kingdoms may rise, kingdoms may fall
Nations refuse to hear God's call
But the Word of the Lord endureth for evermore.
Things that we love last for a day
Then in the morning fade away,
But the Word of the Lord endureth for evermore.
Take God at His promise
Put your faith in Christ;
Trust Him for salvation
And Eternal Life!
Things that we love last for a day
Then in the morning fade away,
But the Word of the Lord endureth for evermore.
© J. Lorimer Gray and D. Kennedy 1969 *By kind permission*

240

1 What a Friend we have in Jesus,
All our sins and griefs to bear!
What a privilege to carry
Everything to God in prayer!
O what peace we often forfeit,
O what needless pain we bear,
All because we do not carry
Everything to God in prayer!

2 Have we trials and temptations?
Is there trouble anywhere?
We should never be discouraged:
Take it to the Lord in prayer.
Can we find a friend so faithful,
Who will all our sorrows share?
Jesus knows our every weakness:
Take it to the Lord in prayer.

3 Are we weak and heavy-laden,
Cumbered with a load of care?
Jesus only is our refuge:
Take it to the Lord in prayer.
Do thy friends despise, forsake thee?
Take it to the Lord in prayer;
In His arms He'll take and shield thee!
Thou wilt find a solace there.

4 What a Friend we have in Jesus,
All our sins and griefs to bear!
What a privilege to carry
Everything to God in prayer!
O what peace we often forfeit,
O what needless pain we bear,
All because we do not carry
Everything to God in prayer!

241

In the stillness of the morning,
May Thy voice alone be heard;
In the quietness of Thy presence
May we hear God's living Word.
In the oneness of the Spirit
We would wait upon Thee, Lord;
In the stillness of the morning,
May Thy blessing be outpoured.
© G. Brattle 1969 *By kind permission*

242

1   What He wants me, He can make me.
    Where He wants me, He can take me,
    But He never will forsake me,
    For I am His own.
    Now my life belongs to Jesus,
    I am His and He is mine.

2   Gracious Lord who died to save me,
    Bore my sins, in love forgave me,
    Life and joy and peace He gave me,
    For I am His own.
    Now my life belongs to Jesus,
    I am His and He is mine.

3   In His mercy Jesus needs me,
    With the light of heaven He leads me,
    With the Bread of Life He feeds me,
    For I am His own.
    Now my life belongs to Jesus,
    I am His and He is mine.

© N. L. Warren 1969   *By kind permission*

243

Start with Refrain
Now this is just the reason why I'm telling you
To present yourselves, give your lives to God
To be a living sacrifice that's holy
And acceptable unto Him.

1   Just think of all that His love has done for
      you,
    Just think of all that His love has done for
      you,
    Just think of all that His love could do still
      through you.
      Refrain

2   He sent His Son and He sent Him just for you,
    Who gave His life, and He gave it all for you
    Just think of all that His love would do yet
      for you.
      Refrain

© J. H. Coulson 1969   *By kind permission*

244

1 'Bow down, be like all the rest!'
   So Daniel's friends were told.
   Dauntless they faced the final test
   God brought them through that fire like gold.
'Don't let the world around squeeze you into
   that same old mould,
Let God remould your lives from within.'
All through His Word it's told how God makes
   us free and bold
To stand life's pressures, without giving in.

2 Single, David faced the giant,
   Faith backed the stone he threw
   Hear, too, Jonathan defiant—
   'God saves by many or by few!'
'Don't let the world around squeeze you into
   that same old mould,
Let God remould your lives from within.'
Why fight the fight alone, claim strength from
   God's own Son,
Whether by few or many He'll win.

3 Samson, though a mighty giant
   And man of God it seems,
   Though called to serve the Lord his God
   Falls before Delilah's schemes.
'Don't let the world around squeeze you into
   that same old mould,
Let God remould your lives from within.'
Don't let them, friend or foe, draw you from
   the one you know,
Stay close to Jesus through thick or thin.

4 Joseph, just a slave to sell,
   Gideon, poor farmer's boy,
   Rebekah, working at the well—
   For each fulfilment was God's plan.
'Don't let the world around squeeze you into
   that same old mould,
Let God remould your lives from within.'
Obey His gracious Word, in everything make
   Him Lord,
Run the straight race with eyes fixed on Him.

© J. H. Coulson 1969 *By kind permission*

245

1 If I tried to live for You Lord, today,
   If I tried to follow Your wonderful way,
   Then all of my life would be me and not You
   And none of Your glory would ever shine
       through.

2 Since I first met You, I knew Lord You were the
       way,
   I tried hard to walk in Your footsteps each day,
   But somehow my life didn't glorify Thee,
   So make me a channel, and You live through
       me.

3 Take each new day, whatever's in store,
   Take my whole being and into me pour,
   Your power, and Your Spirit, Oh make me
       anew,
   For no one can change me, Lord Jesus, but
       You.
   © D. Simmons 1969 *By kind permission*

246

1 Just as I am, without one plea
   But that Thy blood was shed for me,
   And that Thou bidd'st me come to Thee,
   O Lamb of God, I come.

2 Just as I am, poor, wretched, blind,
   Sight, riches, healing of the mind,
   Yea, all I need, in Thee to find,
   O Lamb of God, I come.

3 Just as I am, Thou wilt receive,
   Wilt welcome, pardon, cleanse, relieve;
   Because Thy promise I believe,
   O Lamb of God, I come.

4 Just as I am—Thy love unknown
   Has broken every barrier down—
   Now to be Thine, yea, Thine alone,
   O Lamb of God, I come.

5 Just as I am, of that free love
   The breadth, length, depth, and height to prove,
   Here for a season, then above,
   O Lamb of God, I come.

247

1 Jesus, grant that we may follow
   In our lives, the steps You trod;
   With your life our inspiration
   And our pattern, Son of God.
   Master, teach us how to follow
   On the road to Calvary.
   May Your mind be formed among us,
   From self-interest set us free.

2 Lord we know we cannot follow
   Till You save us from our sin.
   May the fullness of Your Spirit
   Give us risen power within.
   Saviour, give us strength to follow
   Your example and Your law;
   Loving You above all others,
   Others may we love the more.

3 Jesus, give us faith to follow
   Through affliction, pain, and toil.
   In the dangerous times of plenty
   Keep us faithful, true and loyal.
   Peace in turmoil, strength in testing,
   Patience in the slower hours;
   Joy in life and love in all things,
   These were Yours—Lord, make them ours.

© J. Young 1969   *By kind permission*

248

1 I know the Lord is leading me
   He knows my path and destiny
   In every problem of my life He guides me
   I know the Lord is leading me.

2 It is the Saviour leading me.
   Who rose from death triumphantly
   To whom all power in heaven and earth is given
   It is the Saviour leading me.

3 I trust my God in leading me
   Who said all things will work to be
   For good to those He calls, who love Him truly
   I trust my God in leading me.

© Gustav Bosse Verlag   *By kind permission*

249

1 The Lord is near you, right by your side.
He'll never leave you, He is your Guide.
Through doubt and sadness,
In trials and loneliness,
The Lord is near you, right by your side.

2 The Lord will live in you, right in your heart.
His peace He'll give you, His love impart.
He will cleanse your sin away
He will teach you how to pray
When Jesus lives in you, right in your heart.

3 The Lord will come for you, at that Last Day.
When heaven will open its shining way.
Will you be ready then?
Will you be trusting Him?
When Jesus comes again, at that Last Day.
The Lord is near you, right by your side.

© N. L. Warren 1968 *By kind permission*

250

1 I will follow wherever He leads.
Ev'ry problem my Saviour He knows:
Though the path may be long, with His help
I'll be strong,
I will go just wherever He goes.

2 He may lead me to countries where troubles
surround;
Even there He'll be with me, I know
I promise I'll follow wherever Christ leads me,
and so,
I will go just wherever He goes.

3 When the sun starts to set in the sky,
I shall know that I'm nearer my home:
But until the great day,
I shall still trust and pray.
And I'll go just wherever He goes.

© The Four Kingsmen and Cornelius Edition 1968
By kind permission. All rights reserved

251

If you know the Lord,
You need nobody else,
To see you through the darkest night.
You can walk alone,
You only need the Lord,
He'll keep you on the road marked right.
Take time to pray ev'ry day,
And when you're headin' home,
He'll show you the way.
If you know the Lord,
You need nobody else, to see the light,
His wonderful light.

252

1 My Lord's in charge of my life, my life
My Lord's in charge of my life
He knows what is the best for me,
And God's in charge of my life.

2 I put my life in His hands, His hands
I put my life in His hands,
A slave to Him I am fully free
I put my life in His hands.

3 He's got a wonderful plan for me
He's got a wonderful plan
My future's safe though I cannot see
For He's got a wonderful plan.

4 I'll trust my wonderful Lord, my Lord
I'll trust my wonderful Lord,
He cannot fail and He cares for me,
I'll trust my wonderful Lord.

253

1 Happy, those who know they're poor,
For the Kingdom now is theirs;
Happy, those whose grief is sore
For God will wipe away their tears.

2 Happy, those who are the meek,
   They'll inherit all the earth;
   Happy, those who truly seek
   And hunger for His righteousness and worth.

3 For the Saviour whom they know,
   Always satisfies their heart;
   Happy those who mercy show,
   For they'll obtain God's mercy for their part.

4 Happy, you, the pure in heart,
   You will see God in His heaven;
   Happy, too, the folk whose lot
   It is to bring true peace to men.

5 This great blessing shall be theirs,
   In the glory soon to come;
   They shall all be called God's heirs,
   When God our Father calls us to His home.

6 Happy, now you are when men
   Speak against you for My cause;
   You shall have a place in heaven,
   And great reward shall then be yours.
   © C. Blissard-Barnes *By kind permission*

254

1 It's not an easy road we are travelling to
      heaven,
   For many are the thorns on the way;
   It's not an easy road but the Saviour is with us,
   His presence gives us joy ev'ry day.
      Chorus
      No, no, it's not an easy road,
      No, no, it's not an easy road,
      But Jesus walks beside me and brightens the
         journey and lightens ev'ry heavy load.

2 It's not an easy road, there are trials and
      troubles
   And many are the dangers we meet;
   But Jesus guards and keeps so that nothing can
      harm us
   And smooths the rugged path for our feet.
      Chorus.

3 Though I am often footsore and weary from
travel.
Though I am often bowed down with care;
A better day is coming when home in the
glory
I'll rest in perfect peace over there.
Chorus

255

1 While travelling on the heavenly way
I know I'll always need
God's precious Word, which is my sword,
And prayer which is my shield.
My Saviour's presence keeps and guides
Throughout each passing day
I'll never fear the pathway
Along that heavenly way.

2 He's always there beside me
On every mountain side
All thoughts of stumbling flee from me
With Jesus as my guide.
For every footstep that I take
I know He took before
My only wish along the way
Is that I'll know Him more.

3 I read my Bible on the way
To keep me on the road
For if I falter either way
Many snares abound.
I keep in touch with Him by prayer
To keep me free from sin.
I long for that tremendous day
When I can be with Him.

4 For at the end of this same road
There is a place, He said,
Prepared for those who trust in Him
Risen from the dead.
'Worthy the Lamb' my lips will cry
When I before Him come
For ever in His family
When I arrive at home.

256

My sheep hear my voice and I know them and they
  follow me,
And they follow me,
My sheep hear my voice and I know them and they
  follow me.
And I give unto them eternal life and they shall
  never perish.
Neither shall any man pluck them out of my hand
  Repeat 1st 3 lines.

257

1 These chains are invisible
   But these chains are real—
   The chains of sin as strong as steel:
     As strong as steel
     —You can't see—
     Chains of sin
     Holding me.
   Invisible chains holding me fast—
   How long, my Lord, shall this bondage last?

2 God's power is visible,
   And God's power is real—
   The power of love stronger than steel:
     Stronger than steel—
     Can't you see?—
     Power of Love
     Sets me free.
   Invisible chains holding me fast
   —And now, my Lord, is my bondage past?

3 God's chains are invisible,
   God's chains are real—
   Chains of love stronger than steel:
     Stronger than steel
     —You can see—
     Chains of Love
     Holding me free.
   Invisible chains, holding me fast
   —Forever, Lord, may this freedom last!
© P. Monk 1969 *By kind permission*

258

Start with Chorus
Each new day, Lord,
I give it back into Your hands for You gave
it to me
You, my Lord, are the source of time and of
its ending,
I am trusting You.

1   When the shadows gather over the world
Into fear of living I'm frequently hurled
Then You make darkness light.
    Chorus

2   When a day is finished and I look back
I have often failed You—with sins that are black
Yet You cleanse me, O Lord.
    Chorus

3   Many words would have been—better unsaid,
Hardly any thanking—but grumbling instead,
Lord You know what I'm like.
    Chorus

4   Life is all so pointless, lived without You,
Yet You give it purpose when You're leading
me.
My path you know, O Lord.
    Chorus

© Gustav Bosse Verlag, Germany *By kind permission*

259

1   Dark was my night without You Lord.
Long was that never-ending track.
Thank You for finding me.
Thank You for guiding me.
But please don't ever let me look back.

2   Long were those years of my blindness,
Strong were those chains across my back.
Thank You for saving me.
Thank You for loving me.
But please don't ever let me look back.

3 This life You've given me isn't easy.
   But Lord I know it's the best.
   Help me to conquer my temptations
   And guide me as I work and as I rest.

   Repeat Verse 1

© C. Burns *By kind permission*

260

1 We shall overcome,
   We shall overcome,
   We shall overcome some day;
   By faith in Christ I do believe
   We shall overcome some day.

2 The truth will make us free,
   The truth will make us free,
   The truth will make us free some day;
   By faith in Christ I do believe
   We shall overcome some day.

3 The Lord will see us through,
   The Lord will see us through,
   The Lord will see us through some day;
   By faith in Christ I do believe
   We shall overcome some day.

4 We shall live in peace,
   We shall live in peace,
   We shall live in peace some day;
   By faith in Christ I do believe
   We shall overcome some day.

5 We shall overcome,
   We shall overcome,
   We shall overcome some day;
   By faith in Christ I do believe
   We shall overcome some day.

261

1 I had lost my way; there was not a ray of hope
   Life was dark; I could not see an answer.

   Meaningless and blue. What was I to do with
      life?
   Nowhere that I looked was there an answer.

2   I tried all the things that they say
       Give a meaning to living.

       But the more that I took them I found
       Nothing there worth the giving.

3   Then I heard of One, who was God's own Son,
       He had come to earth to be the answer.

       He was crucified. In my place He died.
       So He is the One who gives the answer.

4   Oh Lord—what could I do?
       I saw that I needed You.

       He forgave my sin; now His life's within.
       And I know the Christ who is the answer.

262

1   I was a sinner lonely and sad,
       Jesus came to me and He made me glad,
       Now He has found me His peace does surround
         me
       You need Him too, oh yes; you need Him too,
         oh yes;
       You need Him too.

2   The peace that He gave me was bought on a
         cross,
       He brought me salvation from suffering and loss
       He died to save me, His own life He gave me
       You need Him too, oh yes; you need Him too,
         oh yes;
       You need Him too.

3   He gives me power to overcome sin,
       He gives me His peace and victory within,
       My Saviour protects me, His purpose directs me
       You need Him too, oh yes; you need Him too,
         oh yes;
       You need Him too.

263

1 If you ask me how I know
That Jesus Christ is real
I'll tell you that I trust His Word
And not just what I feel.
    He came to me, He lives in me,
    He fills my heart with love.
    I know Him as my Living Friend
    Who leads me on to Heaven above.

2 If you ask me how I know
My sins are all forgiven
I'll tell you how my Saviour died
To pave my way to Heaven.
    He suffered there in lonely pain,
    Cut off from God for me.
    He took the burden of my guilt,
    He died alone to set me free.

3 If you ask me how I know
There's life beyond the grave
I'll tell you, Jesus rose again
Victorious to save.
    He came to me, He lives in me,
    He fills my heart with love.
    I know Him as my Living Friend
    Who leads me on to Heaven above.

© N. L. Warren 1969 *By kind permission*

264

1 A pilgrim was I and wand'ring,
In the cold night of sin I did roam
When Jesus the kind Shepherd found me,
And now I am on my way home.

    Chorus
    Surely goodness and mercy shall follow me
    All the days, all the days of my life;
    Surely goodness and mercy shall follow me
    All the days, all the days of my life.
    And I shall dwell in the House of the Lord
       forever,
    And I shall feast at the table spread for me;
    Surely goodness and mercy shall follow me
    All the days, all the days of my life.

2 He restoreth my soul when I'm weary,
   He giveth me strength day by day;
   He leads me beside the still waters,
   He guards me each step of the way.
     Chorus

3 When I walk through the dark lonesome valley,
   My Saviour will walk with me there;
   And safely His great hand will lead me
   To the mansions He's gone to prepare.
     Chorus

265

1 O happy day! that fixed my choice
   On Thee, my Saviour and my God!
   Well may this glowing heart rejoice,
   And tell its raptures all abroad.
     Chorus
     O happy day, O happy day,
     When Jesus washed my sins away;
     He taught me how to watch and pray,
     And live rejoicing ev'ry day;
     O happy day, O happy day,
     When Jesus washed my sins away.

2 'Tis done, the great transaction's done!
   I am my Lord's, and He is mine!
   He drew me, and I followed on,
   Charmed to confess the voice divine.
     Chorus

3 Now rest, my long divided heart,
   Fixed on this blissful centre, rest;
   Nor ever from thy Lord depart,
   With Him of ev'ry good possessed.
     Chorus

4 High heav'n, that heard the solemn vow,
   That vow renewed shall daily hear;
   Till in life's latest hour I bow,
   And bless in death a bond so dear.
     Chorus

266

1 My Lord is real, He lives in my soul
  My Lord is real, for He's made me whole;
  He took away my sin and shame,
  Hallelujah to His name.

2 Trust and believe is what you must do,
  And His Spirit will come unto you
  Guide you in His perfect way
  Till He comes again one day.

3 The Lord will judge us when He comes
  And we'll stand righteous in the Son
  No condemnation now we fear
  With Jesus ever near.
  No condemnation now we fear
  With Jesus ever near.
  © N. T. Faithfull *By kind permission*

267

  Start with chorus
  For me to live is Christ, to die is gain,
  To hold His hand, and walk His narrow way
  There is no peace, no joy, no thrill,
  Like walking in His will,
  For me to live is Christ, to die is gain.

1 Now once my heart was full of sin and shame
  Till someone told me Jesus came to save,
  When He said 'Come home to Me',
  He set my poor heart free
  For me to live is Christ, to die is gain.
    Chorus

2 Now there are things that I still do not know
  But of this one thing I'm completely sure:
  He who called me on that day,
  Washed all my sin away,
  For me to live is Christ, to die is gain.
    Chorus
  © J. White *By kind permission*

268

1 I've got a song in my heart. A melody,
   And it's been there since my Lord set me free,
   And there's such peace in my heart
   That I can scarce believe it's real.

2 Joy in my life, I want to tell you
   There's no struggle, no strife
   And it was Christ above alone paid the price,
   When He died on Calvary.

269

My story so sad,
Wand'rin' down life's empty road,
Having such a heavy load to bear,
Didn't know someone was there,
Waiting for me . . .
I'd gone my way,
Tried to find what happiness I could
A hopeless pathway it seems I've trod,
Didn't know someone was there,
Waiting for me.

    Chorus
    Many years spent my way,
    Jesus waited for me,
    When I heard of new life in Him,
    I found the meaning of Calvary.

Now He's mine,
Saviour and my King,
Lord of all,
My life my everything,
I'm so glad,
When I came to Him,
He waited, waited for me.

    Chorus

Now I sing,
Of Salvation's plan,
How it's free,
And for everyone,
Seek Him now,
Jesus Christ, the Son,
He's waiting, waiting for you.
He's waiting for you.

270

1 Hustle, bustle, all day long,
   In this world around us.
   Something, somewhere has gone wrong
   Where d'you think you're going to?

2 Got to keep up with the Jones,
   Things are so important!
   Spending money, getting loans,
   Where d'you think you're going to?

3 What are your priorities?
   Who d'you really want to please?
   Living in this world today,
   People seem to lose their way, Oh!

4 Jesus said 'I am the Way',
   Won't you listen to Him?
   For His words apply today
   Where d'you think you're going to?

5 If you really put Him first,
   Take Him as your Lord and guide,
   He will give you life that's real
   Life that springs afresh inside, Oh!

6 Jesus said 'I am the Way',
   Won't you listen to Him?
   For His words apply today
   Where d'you think you're going to?

© R. G. Wright and K. Lamming 1969
By kind permission

271

1 Won't you stop and think about the life you're
   tasting?
   Are you really worried 'bout the time you're
   wasting?
   Well, we've come to tell you now,
   Yes, we've come to tell you how,
   How you can redeem the time that you've
   lost.

2   You've been working overtime wasting your
    time.
    You may even think that I'm wasting more
    time.
    As we've come to tell you now,
    Yes, we've come to tell you how.
    How you can redeem the time that you have
    lost.
    Chorus
    Well we agree there's a time for living;
    But can't you see, now's the time to give in?
    We see the time and it's going by each day,
    And there'll come a time when it's all gone
    away.

3   It was sometime in the past Jesus spent His
    time,
    When the skies were overcast, paying for your
    crime.
    And we've come to tell you now,
    Yes, we've come to tell you how,
    How you can redeem the time that you have
    lost.
    Chorus

© Sky Sounds *By kind permission*

272

Let's face it, friends: the world is in such a
mess!
Before life ends, let's start living!

1   Kids that live for kicks know no way to fill the
    emptiness;
    Protest songs are hits—but what are they
    saying?
    They say that we're lost, we're all sitting
    waiting for the bang.
    We all know we're lost, but what's the answer?
    Chorus
    Crazy, mixed-up generation, there is only one
    solution—
    Jesus is the great sensation!
    Won't you stop and think,
    Now you're on the brink?

2   Beats think life's a joke, these long-haired
      cynics of society;
    They don't do a stroke . . . but why should
      they?
    Mum and dad at home have lost control of their
      pride and joy;
    Oh, how they moan! What's the answer?
      Chorus

3   Can you be so blind? You can't see the truth
      about yourself!
    Or don't you mind where you're going?
    Jesus knows it all. He knows your situation
      now.
    Why do you stall when He's the answer?
      Chorus

273

1   There is someone waiting, and He waits so
      patiently,
    To be your friend and take away your sin.
    He waits continually, so patiently,
    He's waiting; Oh, won't you come to Him?

     Chorus
     He doesn't ask that you should know the
      greatest things,
     So come to Him and don't delay.
     Come to Him as you are;
     Remember He's not far away from you,
     He's not far away from you.

2   Why keep Jesus waiting? Don't you know that
      He loves you?
    And He's the answer to your emptiness, my
      friend.
    He waits continually, so patiently,
    Will you say yes? It's worth it in the end!
      Chorus

274

1   See the snow drifting o'er the meadows,
    Gentle death from the dismal grey skies
    Summer's gone, Mother Nature's weeping,
    And her tears turn to ice in her eyes.

2 Man can run from the cold of winter;
   Build a fire with a handful of coal
   But the blaze of a thousand pine trees,
   Never melts all the ice in his soul.

3 Last night I dreamed I was in Galilee
   Alone—I watched for hours that silent sea
   A fisherman's net of twine was lying in the
       sand
   The one that Simon Peter left to take his
       Saviour's hand.

4 Last night I roamed the shores of Galilee
   That net, forgotten there, made sense to me.
   Peter turned his back on all he'd ever known
   To follow one who knew the Way, to make that
       life his own.

5 When the cold seems to be so endless
   Grows a flower, small and weak but alive.
   Spring is here, and the ice is melting.
   'It is finished' cried the Lord as He died.

6 Last night I roamed the shores of Galilee
   That net, forgotten there, made sense to me.
   Peter turned his back on all he'd ever known
   To follow one who knew the Way, to make that
       life his own.

© C. Burns   *By kind permission*

275

It's a long, long, long and lonely journey
It's a long, long, long and lonely road.
You need help to lighten your burden
You need help to carry that load.
So give your life to the Lord
Give your life to the Lord
And you'll know how it feels
To be loved as you go.
On that glorious, everlasting journey
On that glorious, never ending road.

© C. Burns   *By kind permission*

276

1 Your fancy clothes, the way you wear your hair.
    You cherish those, you say you really care.
    But when the moth and rust come,
    The dirt and the dust come
    You'll want to hide, there won't be anywhere.

2 You buy a car, you keep it shining bright.
    On your guitar, the label is just right.
    But when the night and fear come,
    And you feel a tear come
    You'll want a friend, there won't be one in
      sight.

3 You're smiling now, but round the corner's
      pain.
    You wonder how you'll ever laugh again.
    Then you'll remember, slowly,
    The things that I told you
    About my Lord, and all that He has said.

© G. McClelland *By kind permission*

277

1 Listen to the story of the little candle,
    Just a little story but the tale is ample
    Lets you know what I mean, maybe too what
      you mean
    When we talk of living and of living to the full.

2 Stands the little candle in a darken'd window,
    Tho' it has potential by itself it won't glow
    Till a lighted taper gently shines upon it,
    Touches it and passes on the light which it
      has on it.

3 Now that little candle lights the darken'd
      window,
    Shines for people outside, glows on people in
      too
    Just a tiny candle with its little glimmer,
    Yet the light is seen for quite a way around.

4 We are just like candles, someone needs to
      light us,
    We have the potential, someone needs to
      guide us:
    Jesus light our darkness, use us for your glory,
    Shining as the candle in the story.

© G. McClelland *By kind permission*

278

1 Down from His glory the Saviour came,
   Into a world of sin and shame,
   Seeking men to love His Father's name,
   'Come unto me'.

   Chorus
   He is our Saviour, our guide and friend,
   He is the one on whom we can depend,
   He is our only hope, world without end.
   'We must believe'.

2 Jesus, the perfect one was humble and kind,
   Healing the halt, the lame and the blind—
   Such power could conquer sin, renew the mind,
   'Follow thou me'.
   Chorus

3 Rich, yet for our sakes He became poor,
   He's our example for evermore.
   God's love in all of us means peace not war,
   'Abide in me'.
   Chorus

4 If we are Christ's, and take the Spirit's sword,
   One day we shall see our blessed Lord,
   What exultation in that glad reward,
   'Rejoice with me'.
   Chorus

5 Learning to live with Christ on this earth below,
   Finding a purpose the world cannot know,
   Looking to Jesus till our lives o'erflow
   'With charity'.
   Chorus

© D. Lowe   *By kind permission*

279

1 If access to heaven depended on you,
   On the number of good deeds you'd done;
   What a wonderful picture you'd paint of
      yourself—
   I'm quite sure you'd rate second to none.

2 But God's not concerned with the things you've
      achieved,
   Though these things may be many or few;
   There's only one way by which men may
      reach God,
   And that doesn't mean all men but you.

3   Jesus said I'm the Way and the Truth and the
    Life,
    No man cometh to God but by Me;
    And that way back to God is to trust in the
    Blood
    That was shed for you—at Calvary.

4   It is Christ's Blood alone that has power to
    cleanse
    From the dire consequences of sin;
    And it's only on seeing that sin-cleansing Blood
    That the Father will say 'Enter in; Enter in'.

5   All have sinned and fall short of the glory of
    God,
    And the Bible has made it quite plain—
    That your righteousnesses are to Him filthy
    rags,
    If you think they'll avail, think again.
    Think again—Think again—Think again.

280

Start with chorus
Have you ever wished you knew how to pray?
Have you ever wished you knew what to say?
Do you ever wonder why you're alive?
Do you ever wish you knew?
I know you do.

1   I've found the answer for a lonely empty heart;
    Take Jesus in your life and make another start.
    Oh people! Listen all you people!
    Chorus

2   I've found the answer for a lonely empty soul;
    Take Jesus in your life and He will make you
    whole.
    Oh people! Listen all you people!

    Chorus
    Anybody saved can learn how to pray
    Anybody saved can know what to say
    Anybody saved knows why he's alive
    Do you ever wish you knew?
    I know you do.

281

1 The Lord is my friend and on Him I depend
  He guides us on our way and forever with us
    will stay,
  If we trust, trust in Him, He will lead us every
    day.

2 One thing is required that we trust in our God.
  For He died on the tree to set us all free
  From the bond of our sin, just simply believe
    in Him.

3 Come now to the cross with your faith small
    and weak,
  He will help you to believe if only Him you'll
    seek.
  He will come in to your heart and He'll reign
    in every part.

4 The Lord is my friend and on Him I depend
  He guides us on our way and forever with us
    will stay,
  If we trust, trust in Him, He will lead us every
    day.
© A. Winkworth *By kind permission*

282

1 I have got a friend that's true
  Someone who will see me through,
  He guides me in all I do—
  His Name is Jesus.
  When I stumble He is there, all my troubles
    He will share.
  He's the Saviour, the One who cares—His
    Name is Jesus.
  However great the storm He will make the
    waters calm,
  And through the darkest night Jesus is the
    guiding light.
  I find comfort when I read of the things He's
    done for me.
  Yes, I've got a Friend indeed—His Name is
    Jesus—His Name is Jesus.

2   When the road seems hard and long and things
      keep on going wrong,
    Someone always makes me strong, His Name
      is Jesus.
    Sometimes on life's restless waves I'm a ship
      without a sail,
    But my Captain will never fail, His Name is
      Jesus.
    The joy that He imparts brings a warmness to
      my heart
    That's far beyond compare to the earthly joys
      I share!
    While I walk and talk with Him all my battles
      He will win,
    He helps me in everything, His Name is Jesus,
      His Name is Jesus.

3   Friends around me, young and old, don't be
      orphans in the cold,
    Come to One who loves you so, His Name is
      Jesus.
    Earthly treasures you possess won't give deep
      down happiness,
    Only One ever will do that, His Name is Jesus.
    This modern world today soon can lead your
      heart astray,
    There's so much sin and strife creeping into
      every life.
    Yet there's one sure way you can overcome the
      Devil's plan,
    Put your faith and trust in One, His Name is
      Jesus, His Name is Jesus.

© D. Drinkall *By kind permission*

283

1   Joe's my friend and he thought I was mad,
    And he used to work so hard, in the office
      near the yard,
    And he was working nine till five, thinking
      money all the time,
    And now he knows, knows he was wrong.

Chorus
Jesus says 'I am the Way, the Truth and
the Life
And with me will you only find Light.'
He died for me; I died with Him and so my
life has changed
And my world will never be the same.

2 Joe then thought, 'Now I'll work for the poor,'
   And he used to give his time to the people who
   were blind,
   And he was searching for some point to give
   purpose to his life,
   And now he knows, knows that's not enough
                                   Chorus

3 Then one day when his mood was so sad,
   For he'd given up all hope and his footsteps
   were so slow,
   But then he saw a smiling man who placed a
   booklet in his hand
   And then he read, read what it said.

   Jesus says 'I am the Way, the Truth and the
   Life
   And with me will you only find Light-
   He died for Joe; he died with Him and so
   his life has changed
   And his world can never be the same.

4 Yes, he's changed quite beyond all belief,
   And he likes to work so hard, in the office near
   the yard,
   And he has found a new life now, thinks the
   world of the Lord,
   Because he knows, knows what is life.
   Because he knows the Lord is living in him.

   Jesus says, 'I am the Way, the Truth and the
   Life
   And with me will you only find Light.'
   He died for you; please die with Him,
   And then your life will change
   And your world will never be the same
   And your world will never be the same.

284

1 Long ago, when Rome ruled half the earth
  Lived a man who came of humble birth
  He said His Father reigned in Heav'n above
  Does His claim ring true?

2 Crowds would follow everywhere He went
  And He told them why He had been sent
  To save the world through God's redeeming
    love
  Does His claim ring true?
    Hear this mighty Jew
    Does His claim ring true?

3 Was He just a man who'd lost His mind
  Was He just a fraud, yet you will find
  That He healed the sick and cured the blind
  Does His claim ring true?
    Hear Him for He said
    I will rise from the dead.

4 Was He just a man who'd lost His mind?
  Was He just a fraud? yet you will find
  That His Church was born because it knew
  That His claim rings true.

285

1 Figured out some time ago, life was just a road,
  As I wandered through the years,
  Heavy grew my load,
  Sometimes people passed me by
  I'd ask them where they're going,
  Always they'd say we don't know,
  Our wild oats we've got to sow,
  Don't ask questions, just you keep on going.

2 So I journeyed down the road,
  The only one I'm knowing,
  Soon my burdens and my cares
  On me began a-showing,
  In despair to God I cried,
  Please hear what I'm saying,
  Can't you show me some way out,
  Though I haven't any doubt
  I just didn't know what I was saying.

3   Then one day I saw a man,
     On another highway,
     Called to me across the stream,
     Are you going my way?
     I said thanks I don't think so,
     Why should I change direction,
     He said listen change your mind,
     Can't you see that corner's blind
     Please don't wait too long
     Please don't wait too long before correction.

4   I said okay, what's your name,
     He told me it was Jesus,
     Told me that the road I'm on
     The devil made to keep us,
     Reaching out across the stream
     He said you'll have to trust me,
     As I reached His outstretched hand
     I suddenly could understand
     This could be no ordinary man.

     Now with Jesus by my side,
     I'm on the other highway,
     Now I call to all my friends,
     Are you going my way?
     Are you going my way?

© V. Howard and P. Howard
By kind permission

286

1   One night I had a dream,
     Through a swirling fog I walked alone
     By the edge of a stream
     I heard somebody groan,
     I stopped and looked into a pool
     And saw the reflection of a fool,
     And saw the reflection of a fool.

2   Dragging him by his throat
     Were the collar and the links of a chain,
     On his shoulders a coat,
     On his feet shoes of pain.
     The coat was strife, the chain was pride,
     I saw the reflection and I cried,
     I saw the reflection and I cried,

3   Tears for myself, the fool,
    A man chained by independence,
    Gripped by despair so cruel
    My life was a lot of nonsense,
    My eyes were closed, but in my mind
    I saw the reflection so unkind,
    I saw the reflection so unkind

4   Sick of life, scared of death,
    My days just one long futility.
    Seeing my emptiness
    I cried, 'God make me free'.
    I looked once more, I don't know how,
    And saw the reflection changing now,
    And saw the reflection changing now.

5   A man was in my place.
    A man with holes in His hands and side,
    A man I could not face,
    The man I had crucified,
    On Him was my coat, my chains and my shoes,
    And between reflections I must choose,
    Between reflections I must choose.

287

1   A boy once sat by the side of the river
    Dipping his feet in the cool, cool water
    He watched the little fishes a'lazily swimming
        by.
    He looked up into the blue, blue heaven,
    He saw the birds and he started to question,
    Who he was, where he was, what he was, and
        why?
    And he found no answer in the blue heaven
    Or the lazy fishes or the birdies in the sky.

2   He'd heard about a book and they call'd it the
        Bible,
    And some folks said it was only a fable,
    But no-one else could tell him how to live or
        what would happen when he died.
    So he read, at the start ev'rything had been
        perfect,

But changes had come through a man's
disobedience,
But God still lov'd him so He sent His Son to
to suffer and die.
And he marvell'd at a God who lov'd the
birds and the fishes
And yet sent His only loving Son to suffer
and to die.

3 What could he do now to gain God's affection
How could his life take a brand new direction
He wondered in his heart just exactly where
the answer did lie.
So he got down on his knees and he ask'd for
forgiveness.
And when he'd confess'd, well, he wanted to
witness,
He shouted to the fishes in the stream and the
birdies in the sky.
And Christ was the answer to the who, and
the where, and the what, and the how, and
the answer to the why.

© G. McClelland *By kind permission*

288

1 There's a time to reap, a time to sow,
That seeds planted every day will grow,
And oh, didn't you know,
The Bible tells me so.

2 There's a time to laugh, a time to cry,
A time to live and a time to die,
I know; didn't you know,
The Bible tells me so.

3 The good Lord watches over everyone,
Every day and night.
He made the sun and He made the moon
So the future would be bright.

4 There's a time to reap, a time to sow,
A time to pray when the evening lights
Are low, didn't you know,
The Bible tells me so.

289

1   Think of tomorrow, what will it bring you?
    How can you face it all alone?
    Though ev'rything seems fine
    Tomorrow is a long, long, time.
    The Lord said There is no man or woman
    That cannot find a place in His love
    And there is no sin that's bigger than His mercy
    So there's a place for you in heav'n above.

2   Whoever hears His knock upon their heart's
        door
    However faint that knocking might be
    You can be sure His arms will be wide open
    And there's a place for you and a place for me.
    Think of tomorrow, what will it bring you?
    How can you face it all alone?
    Though ev'rything seems fine
    Tomorrow is a long, long, time.

290

1   Do you know about Jesus born in stable bare?
    Do you know about Jesus coming down His
        love to share?
    Do you know about Jesus or don't you really
        care?
    Do you know about my Lord?

2   Do you know about my Saviour who died on
        Calvary?
    Do you know about my Saviour hanging there
        in agony?
    Do you know about my Saviour who loves
        you and me?
    Do you know about my Lord?

3   Now today we hear a lot about the atom
        bomb and things,
    Have you any time to think about the peace
        that Jesus brings?
    Do you listen to the Christian who of his
        Saviour sings?
    Do you know about my Lord?

291

1 We're in a great race to put rockets in space,
   But the needs of our souls we're refusing to
      face;
   I search myself through for a purpose that's
      true,
   For life is one frantic chase.
      Chorus
      Someone tell me the way
      I'm lost and needing to know;
      The tangles of doubt and what life is about;
      What answer can anyone show?

2 There are Minis and Jags and plenty of fags,
   And money comes easy without many snags,
   Position to win, with a pension thrown in,
   But life is empty, and drags.
      Chorus

3 As a kid I was given one free day in seven,
   With bangers for breakfast and church at
      eleven;
   Now a garden I weed, Sunday scandal I read,
   Clean car, but no thought of Heaven.
      Chorus

4 To conform is the way in the world of today,
   A world of sick humour and moral decay;
   Love's easy and free, the experts agree,
   But life is swinging away.
      Chorus

5 If God could just dwell on earth for a spell,
   A God who could save from the boredom of
      hell;
   And if pain could be shared by a Saviour who
      cared,
   Then why does nobody tell?
      Chorus

© R. T. Bewes 1969 *By kind permission*

292

> Start with Chorus
> *My soul is a witness for my Lord, my soul*
> *is a witness for my Lord*
> *Oh! My soul is a witness for my Lord, my*
> *soul is a witness for my Lord.*

1   You read in the Bible and you understand,
      Methuselah was the oldest man;
  He lived nine`hundred and sixty nine, and he
      died and went to heaven Lord, in-a due time.
  Now, Methuselah was a witness for my Lord,
      Methus'lah was a witness for my Lord.
      Chorus

2   You read in the Bible and you understand,
      Samson was the strongest man;
  Samson went out at one time, an' he killed
      about a thousand of the Philistine.
  O, Samson was a witness for my Lord, Samson
      was a witness for my Lord.
      Chorus

3   Now Daniel was a Hebrew child, he went to
      pray to his God awhile;
  The king at once for Daniel did sen', and he
      put him right down in the lions' den.
  God sent His angels the lions for to keep, an'
      Daniel lay down an' went to sleep.
  Now, Daniel was a witness for my Lord, now
      Daniel was a witness for my Lord.
      Chorus

293

  Start with chorus
  My Lord, what a morning,
  My Lord, what a morning,
  My Lord, what a morning,
  When the stars begin to fall!

1   You'll hear the trumpet sound,
  To wake the nations underground.
  Looking to my Lord's right hand
  When the stars begin to fall!
      Chorus

2   You'll hear the sinners moan
  To wake the nations underground.
  Looking to my Lord's right hand . . .
      Chorus

3   You'll hear the Christians shout
  To wake the nations underground.
  Looking to my Lord's right hand . . .
      Chorus

294

1 Well, early in the morning
About the break of day
I asked the Lord to find the way
Help me find the way to the promised land
This lonely body needs a helping hand
I asked the Lord, won't you help me, please,
Help me find the way.

2 When the new day's a-come
On my bed in prayer
I pray, O Lord, won't you lead me there
Won't you guide me safe to the golden strand
Won't you lead this body; this burden share?
I asked the Lord, won't you help me, please,
Help me find the way.

3 When the judgment comes and the world's in
   chains
And the trumpet blows, won't you call my
   name?
When the thunder rolls, when the heavens
   break
And the sunshine's fire ne'er shines again,
I asked the Lord, won't you help me, please,
Help me find the way.

295

1 O once upon a time a long way back,
A pharoah ruled whose heart was black,
And he had some slaves from the Hebrew land,
Who pulled the stone for the pyramids grand.

   Chorus
   And pull, you Hebrews, pull.
   Pull, you Hebrews, pull.
   It's work all day with nothing for your pay;
   And bury the loser along the way,
   And pull, you Hebrews, pull, and sweat,
      and die!

2 Then Moses came and he said, 'Let be!
The Hebrew people ought to be free.'
So he killed a man to start a war,
But the Hebrews said, 'We want no more!'
   Chorus

3 So Pharoah called for Moses' blood
   Had Hebrews gather straw for their mud.
   And Moses fled to the wilderness,
   'I'll wash my hands of the whole blamed mess.'
   Chorus

4 And God in the wilderness Moses groomed,
   Then spoke from a burning bush not consumed.
   'You go to Egypt, fear not Pharoah,
   And tell him to let my people go.'

   Chorus
   O let my people go.
   Let my people go.
   Who work all day with nothing for their pay;
   And bury the loser along the way,
   O let my people go, from death, and Hell!

5 And Moses came with his fearful rod,
   And Egypt felt the wrath of God.
   In locusts and frogs and lice and blight,
   And first born sons dying all in the night.
   Chorus

6 Then Pharoah rose in his grief and pain,
   And cleared the Hebrews from his domain.
   The Hebrews crossed the wild sea tame,
   And claimed their freedom in God's name.
   Chorus

© E. J. Bash *By kind permission*

296

Start with chorus
Didn't my Lord deliver Daniel, deliver
   Daniel, deliver Daniel?
Didn't my Lord deliver Daniel and why
   not-a every man?

1 He delivered Daniel from the lion's den,
   Jonah from the belly of the whale,
   And the Hebrew children from the fiery furnace
   —and why not-a every man?
   Chorus

2   The wind blows east and the wind blows west,
        it blows like the Judgement Day;
    And every soul that's never prayed is glad to
        a-pray that day.
        Chorus

3   If the moon run down in a purple stream, and
        the sun forbear to shine,
    And the stars in the heavens all disappear,
        King Jesus shall be mine!
        Chorus

297

1   I got a home in-a that Rock, don't you see?
    I got a home in-a that Rock, don't you see?
    Between the earth and sky, thought I heard
        my Saviour cry,
    'You got a home in-a that Rock, don't you see?'

2   Poor man Lazarus, poor as I, don't you see?
    Poor man Lazarus, poor as I, don't you see?
    Poor man Lazarus, poor as I, when he died he
        found a home on high,
    He had a home in-a that Rock, don't you see?

3   Rich man Dives lived so well, don't you see?
    Rich man Dives lived so well, don't you see?
    Rich man Dives lived so well, when he died
        he went to Hell.
    He had no home in-a that Rock, don't you see?

4   God gave Noah the rainbow sign, don't you
        see?
    God gave Noah the rainbow sign, don't you
        see?
    God gave Noah the rainbow sign, no more
        water, but fire next time!
    Better get a home in-a that Rock, don't you
        see?

298

1   'Come to Me, ye who are hard oppressed;
    Lay your head gently upon My breast;
    Come to Me, and I will give you rest;
    Weary one, hither come! God is your home!'

2 'Come to Me!' Jesus now gently pleads.
  'Come to Me! I can supply all needs;
  And My way unto green pastures leads,
  Free from sin! Enter in! God is your home.'

299

1 We are climbing Jacob's ladder
  We are climbing Jacob's ladder
  We are climbing Jacob's ladder
  Soldiers of the Cross

2 Ev'ry rung goes higher 'n' higher
  Ev'ry rung goes higher 'n' higher
  Ev'ry rung goes higher 'n' higher
  Soldier of the Cross.

3 Sinner do you love my Jesus?
  Sinner do you love my Jesus?
  Sinner do you love my Jesus?
  Soldier of the Cross.

4 If you love Him, why not serve Him?
  If you love Him, why not serve Him?
  If you love Him, why not serve Him?
  Soldier of the Cross.

5 Faithful prayer will make a soldier
  Faithful prayer will make a soldier
  Faithful prayer will make a soldier
  Soldier of the Cross.

6 We are climbing higher 'n' higher
  We are climbing higher 'n' higher
  We are climbing higher 'n' higher
  Soldiers of the Cross

An *Index* follows of titles and first lines of all the items in both *Youth Praise* songbooks, that is, numbered 1–299 The first line is included, in italics, only when it differs from the title as given in the music editions.

Index

In the Music editions the choruses and songs have been grouped under the following headings—so that they can be used purposefully rather than 'just for singing'.

MORE FALCONS

Who Was This Man?
Gavin Reid

A clear introduction to what Christians believe about Jesus Christ: who he was and why he is important.

Journey into life
Norman Warren

A basic guide to becoming a Christian, written in a very straightforward style, with frequent helpful pictures and diagrams. Half a million copies sold.

The Case against Christ
John Young

A crisp, easy-to-read clash with popular objections to the Christian faith; faces the challenge of science, the fact of other religions, the trustworthiness of the Bible, and whether God's existence can be proved.

My God is real
David C. K. Watson

This readable book sets out the basics of the Christian gospel as understood by one of Britain's outstanding young preachers.

These and other Falcon books are part of the missionary concern through literature of the Church Pastoral Aid Society, Falcon Court, 32 Fleet Street, London EC4Y 1DB. Send to CPAS for lists of books, leaflets and filmstrips and for information on other aspects of its work.